# Moments of Rising Mist

# Moments of Rising Mist

A Collection of

Sung Landscape Poetry

*translated by*

Amitendranath Tagore

A MUSHINSHA BOOK

GROSSMAN PUBLISHERS

*The illustrations by Yang Po-jun are from a collection published in Shanghai in 1870.*

First published in the United States of America
in 1973 by
GROSSMAN PUBLISHERS, INC.
625 Madison Avenue
New York, N.Y. 10022

Designed and produced by Mushinsha Limited, IRM/Rosei Bldg.
4, Higashi Azabu 1-chome, Minato-ku, Tokyo, Japan
Copyright in Japan, 1973, by Amitendranath Tagore. All rights reserved.
Printed in Japan.
*First Edition,* 1973
*Library of Congress Catalog Card No. 72–90819*

Let my vital force now attain the immortal air;
Now let this body be reduced to ashes.
OM, O my mind,
Remember—remember all that has been done.
Remember—remember all that has been done.
                    *Īśā Upaniṣad*

# *Foreword*

POETRY AND EMOTION are like inseparable friends. In China Confucian codes of behavior curbed outpourings of human emotion and made some ancient scholars and bureaucrats behave like lifeless robots. On the other hand, the veneration that was shown towards Chinese poets makes us believe that that was one way the Chinese people displayed their emotions. The poets were somehow beyond the jurisdiction of court etiquette.

Emotionalism in Chinese poetry came to maturity during the Sung Dynasty (960–1127), and with it the poet's involvement with nature also deepened. The poet no longer stood outside as an observer of nature but considered himself as an integral part of nature. The world of nature has always mystified and vitalized the creative genius of China. In China there has always been an effort to arrive at a harmonious accord between man and nature. This accord emerged from the Chinese faith that to know the position of man in the totality of our universe is the height of wisdom, and one who has achieved it is a sage. Thus sagehood is to be attained not by competing with but by cooperating with nature. This cooperative communication between man and nature was expressed through Shan-shui Shih (Landscape Poetry). The poet seems to convey that his contemplation of landscape is no different from his contemplation of reality. Thus in the best of Chinese landscape poems there is this unanimity between appearance and reality. This is also what Chuang Tzu has termed "Heavenly Identity."

The poems selected for this book appear to have passed that "identity" test. However, I have not translated these poems to prove any literary theory. The only criterion of selection has been one of personal liking. I have been intrigued by the presence of intense nature consciousness in Chinese poets, classical and modern, and the poems were collected to satisfy my own hankering for the world outside my immediate four walls. I offer no other justification for having translated them.

I began to select and translate these poems in Santiniketan, India, in 1963 when I received a Fulbright Alumni Research Grant from the United States Educational Foundation in India. The work came to a halt when I moved to the United States in 1964; I was not able to complete it until my sabbatical in the autumn of 1970. Dr. Jan Yün-hua of McMaster University, Hamilton, Ontario, Canada, helped me in the final selection of the poems; Professor Jerome P. Seaton of the University of North Carolina, Chapel Hill, North Carolina, has been very helpful with his critical suggestions. Marian Wilson's editorial help with the manuscript has been invaluable. I extend my grateful thanks to them. The responsibility for any mistakes is of course mine. However, my friendship with several contemporary Chinese poets has shown me how charitable they are towards their "barbarian" literary collaborators; this encourages me to think that perhaps the souls of Su Shih, Ou-yang Hsiu, Lin Pu and others will smile with benign indulgence at my efforts.

*Amitendranath Tagore*
*Oakland University*
*Rochester, Michigan*

# Contents

# Hsü Hsüan

## I climb the Kan-lu[1] Monastery peak
### and look towards the north

Tide approaches the curved shore of Ching-k'ou[2] and levels the bank.
Wind that rises at Haimen[3] causes the frothy waves.
Strollers on the sand, I watch their shadows.
A boat crosses the river; I can hear the sound of oars.
'Midst the delicate shoots of new grass, view of the distant ferry grows faint.
Smoke hides the city of Kuang-ling.[4]
The homesick traveller thinks of oranges.
When I look up, emotion moves me; I love both places.

## I DABBLE IN THE WATER BY THE BANK
## OF THE RIVER AT CHING-K'OU

I resigned my post, seeking lonesome quiet by the river.
South of the Yangtze it is the spring sky.
A huge blue screen; on it rests Kan-lu Pavilion.
I count the sails; it is a bright day,
The boats move towards the sea.
Limpid ripples flow over shallow stones, jade-cold;
Grass meets the duckweed by the beach;
It is green like fog.
How can I board the boat and sail farther east?
Far from those islands, I dabble in the murmuring current.

## A VILLA AT LU-LUNG VILLAGE ON AN AUTUMN DAY

Reject these worldly cares,
Walk leisurely with village idlers.
Sound of the trees; evening comes to the village inn.
Tinted grass, autumn comes to the old city.
Solitary bird streaks across the sky;
Lazy clouds pass over the dyke.
Don't ask who I am;
The hill, the trees, the empty boat.

## Writing at the Northern Cove of the Fu-kuei Mountains

This is truly a lonely mountain;
Dark precipice gathers a dim blue hue.
Why must there be so many rocks and streams?
They give the impression of a thousand cliffs.
Who could have guessed a place like this, so near?
Morning and evening the air is excellent.
Shadows on the pool tremble in light breeze,
Rain-washed sky freshens the light in the forest.
I stretch on this fragrant grass resting my chin on my hands;
There is enough here to make me forget worldly cares.
I cannot think of going back,[1]
Let me at last live in quiet and peace.

### EVENING SCENE ON THE RIVER IN AUTUMN

Setting sun lights up the flat current,
Clear sky and miles and miles of autumn.
Maple leaves flutter light and bright;
Confused dots are the seagulls.
Fishing net at the end of the pole hangs quiet;
Bamboo hats and umbrellas are gathering paddy.
I dare not indulge the joy of idleness,
Slowly I descend the city tower.

## WITH CH'EN AT CHUANG-HSIN SPRING
## IN THE HSI-MA MOUNTAINS

The door of the mountain lodge is open already; we wait to remove our caps.
Once again we wash our hearts in the cliff spring.
A constant, delicate, faint music comes; the sound of pines.
Suddenly a few petals drop on the high peak;
Water flows over shallow stones unchecked and passes through the sedge path.
Early lights shine through the bamboo forest.
When shall we boil the tea and brew the fragrant wine?
On the sandy ridge we hear the giggling of the night apes.

## WRITING POEMS ON DUCKWEED FLOWERS
### WHILE BOATING ON AN AUTUMN DAY

Natural beauty crowds round the moving boat,
Tender fragrance covers the jade-green stream.
Distant fog is distinct and clear,
Lighter waves make us move slowly.
Rains have stopped, the lake is quiet and full;
Cold wind brings the autumn to the Yangtze.
This dawn, the current sings of places,
Here is the isle of white duckweed.

## WATCHING SCENERY WITH TA-CHIEN[1] CHUNG

### FROM A BOAT

Levee lies athwart the northern slope;
Three trips in a month are not too many.
When an old man visits relatives it is hard to be brief;
There is nothing like the taste of restful leisure.
The traveller crosses the deep-gorge bridge set against a screen of trees;
Village lane, a puff of breeze, the wild song of the herdsman.
Lonely oar, aimless floating, gives a strange joy;
River is full, day is fair, we play with small ripples.

## Gazing at the Chiang Mountain from a boat with Shao-chien[1] Chang

Deep-gorge road goes further back,
Hill facing us is high and heavy.
Scattered trees are wrapped in red leaves;
At times white clouds play with the peak.
The whole day passes, our oars lie still;
In what year was I drunk, resting against a pine?
I know leisure is hard to come by;
I dare not laugh at Chou-yung.[2]

## Once again i write about the river gulls of Pai-lu Island and present the poem to Master Ch'en

Riverside road slopes by the Pai-lu isle;
Light gulls interlock their wings and fill the sandy shore.
I come out to see off my guest leaving for distant lands;
You heave a sigh by the waiting boat.
Wine-shop flags, fishing boats—neither conflicts;
Moon shadows, reed flowers remain in harmony.
Farewell feast and a song clear up all discord;
The company melts the heart; the birds are not alarmed.
Man in his life never knows the joy of water-birds;
We quietly use our useless names in ladies' chambers.
We walk hand in hand thinking of the same thing;
Away from gold tripods and red gravel[1]—how quiet it is!
Beyond the horizon a little danger may lurk;
After this I ought to grow a white mustache.
Sir, I beg you not to forget this place once you leave;
But long protect this fluttering, clean, white beauty.

Lin Pu

## EVENING SCENE FROM THE LAKE TOWER

Water of the lake meets the blue sky,
Leaning on the railing, I grow tired of gazing.
Evening chill, the hills are deep blue,
The autumn is clear, wild geese fly high.
Wandering thoughts reach a thousand miles;
This floating life is light as a hair.
Countless are the trees of the wood;
Sombre clouds screen the fishing boat.

## IDLY DRIFTING ON AN AUTUMN DAY ON WEST LAKE

Fog merges with the mountain shadow,
It is already autumn in this vast expanse.
In the forest I enjoy looking at the monastery,
Shoreline is peaceful. Alas! my boat moves away.
Distant reeds droop with early cold;
A rainbow fragment girdles the evening's end.
Where is my hut?
Pleasure of homecoming rises from the fisherman's song.

# VIEW OF THE NORTHERN MOUNTAIN

In the evening I come to see this mountain's northern view.
Even a painting cannot be like this:
Village lanes, blowing yellow leaves;
Huts appear damp and blue.
Woodcutter[1] is there beyond the clouds;
The monk approaches the water's edge.
Whose flute is playing this tune?
Reeds and rushes, white birds fly.

## WINTER EVENING IN A MOUNTAIN VILLAGE

Grasses grow bent below the sloping forest,
Spring color is already obscured.
Snowy bamboo hangs down in cold blue;
Wind scatters the plum blossoms—a fragrant evening.
A year or more has passed; the recluse has lived alone,
I have not been busy serving tea.
Egrets sometimes rise two by two
And fly wildly across the pond.

## A RECLUSE BY THE LAKE

Lake water enters the bamboo fence,
Mountains surround the cottage.
A recluse's life avoids this world.
The unused door hides behind a green-moss hue;
When a stranger passes, the white birds fly in alarm.
Selling herbs, I taste and compare but charge no price.
I do some gardening, but love to do it unplanned.
Why is the wooded path leading to T'ien-chu[1] monastery
Still in autumn deeply dreaming in blue?

# Mountain retreat at Ch'ih-yang

A cluster of village inns by the mountain slope;
I get off the horse by the rickety bridge. It is evening already.
Frightened birds rush suddenly, parting the dark trees of the gorge;
Shaded flowers lazily fall and a fragrant breeze rises from the dyke.
Idle hours, anchored boat—I especially love them.
In later days, remembering this I shall certainly go mad.
Ah! next moment the sound of a flute!
A wine-flag[1] flutters slightly by the distant bamboo grove.

# The Bamboo Grove

Bamboos by the temple lie athwart,
Pressing close with a thousand tips of green.
Mountain cliffs wear all over
The bark[1] of dry bamboos.
Now I recall your home,
On the whitewashed wall the picture of those plants!

## Mountain pavilion of Master Yi-ts'ung

Edging the forest, it is autumn in the hills,
White birds fly;
Here elegant taste is rare.
West-village ferry. They are late.
I sit and watch
Fishing boats returning in pairs.

## Written while viewing the river in autumn

Egrets asleep on the vast sand-drift,
A strip of water, not a blemish
Soaking the blue sky.
I love most the reed flowers just after the rains.
A sail and smoke;
They are cooking food in the fishing boat.

## ON THE CH'ENG-KUNG BRIDGE

Evening peaks cut across the blue,
Treetops glow red.
Several rows of boats,
Shadows of fishing nets on the water.
I recall that in the South I have seen
Chü-jan's[1] famous painting on a screen.

# Mei Yao-ch'en

## Travelling to Lung-men from Ch'ien-ch'i, I pass by the Pao-ying monastery

From afar I love this beautiful summer view;
It is an active and pure feeling.
How would one know about this whirling stream?
You feel it as you come to the flat ravine.
An ancient temple hidden amid bamboos,
The whole cliff by the shrine is jagged.
Rosy clouds play with the bright clear sky,
Grass and trees have a new green look;
Seasonal yellow birds are here,
Hill flowers struggle in riotous joy.
Speak not of the long road home,
The bright moon returns to her place.

# CLOUDS ON THE MOUNTAIN

A shower passes across the blue sky,
Mountain clouds return to the tallest peaks.
Forest edge hides the rainbow,
Moving shadows descend the stream.
I return to see the parrots fly,
Once more I love this mountain peace.

## I ENJOY A COOL BREEZE IN MING-YÜAN PARK PAVILION
### WITH FRIENDS AND SHARE IN WRITING VERSES

Shoreline is capped in pure cool earth;
Suddenly joy seems boundless.
Shady bamboos after an evening shower;
Forest reveals the remnant of a rainbow.
Dappled shadows rest on quiet waves;
Sound of sutras[1] drifts from east of the low bank.

## Avoiding the summer heat I visit Hsiang-shan Monastery with Hsi-shen

With a friend I climb towards the new sky.
The forest is cloudy; we knock on the door.
A light boat passes the lower ferry,
Distant water floods the forebank.
Marshlands have a shadowy growth;
Mist on the peaks takes on a sombre hue.
Who knows how to obtain these profound tastes?
We tread these ancient rocks green with moss.

## BOATING ON THE EVENING RIVER WITH HSI-SHEN

Floating gently down the calm waves,
Not knowing how far the boat will go.
A gust of wind rises down-river;
We love those clouds on the peak.
Water-birds agree to silence,
Shady growth fills the Island of Reeds. Evening falls;
Last words before returning home are delayed.
Why not row till the moon returns?

# KUNG-LU STREAM

I reach the stream of Duke Yüan;[1]
The broken bank still resembles a ruined fort.
Withered willows stand far out in the nearby bay;
Fresh reeds have just emerged from water.
Sauntering, I approach the ancient pagoda;
Alarmed birds fly in pairs.
From whence comes the sound of fowls and dogs?
People do live in this deep valley.

## FROM MIDDLE CHÜN-CHI HALL I CLIMB THE MAIN PEAK OF T'AI-SHIH[1] MOUNTAIN

I stop the carriage facing the green cliff,
The climbing wistaria knows no fatigue.
People are coming from beyond the trees,
The road spirals up towards the clouds.
Suddenly I feel the fog and the rainbow;
I look back and the peaks are all transformed.

## CROSSING THE CH'ANG-LU[1] RIVER AT DAYBREAK

A sash-like moon over the wintry bank,
Guttering stars dip in the water.
Sails are spread, the wind's course is true;
The boat glides fast, dividing the foam.
Fog across the river is white;
I hear the cock crow from the other bank.
The sky clears and Chien-yeh[2] is near;
Bell Peak towers over the lonely cloud.

## I ASCEND THE CITY RAMPARTS OF CHOU-WANG

### UNDER A FRESH BLUE SKY

I walk on the old city wall,
Having come from afar to see the old city.
Water-birds follow where men live;
The flowing river separates the mulberry and *che*[1] trees.
Autumn hills and a clear blue sky,
The old farmer's time to sow has come.
Disputes among the people are now rare,
Slowly I proceed towards my quiet quarters.

## THE FARMER

Tall trees shade the brushwood door,
Green moss reflects the setting sun.
Shouldering the hoe he watches the mountain moon rise.
Now to find the homeward lane in this misty wilderness,
The old man leans on the boy and strains to see.
The lanky cow returns with her calf.
What food will be served before the lamp?
Shallots are fattening in the dew.

# A Walk on Lu-shan Mountain

My longing for wilderness is satisfied:
Mountains all around, high and low.
There is variety in these wonderful peaks;
I walk alone and lose myself in the dark path.
Hoar frost falls and bears climb the trees.
An empty wood; deer drink from the stream.
Where do the people dwell?
A cock crows once from beyond the clouds.

# RAIN

Spring clouds turn into rain;
The day has darkened a few times.
Swallows are wet but still can fly swiftly;
Flowers are cold, their color deepens.
I hire a cart but I grieve for my guest's departure to a distant land;
Struggling horses are afraid of the mud.
Evening sky clears with a bright light;
Green shadows descend on western windows.

童子抱琴来
卧山青相向
楊伯潤

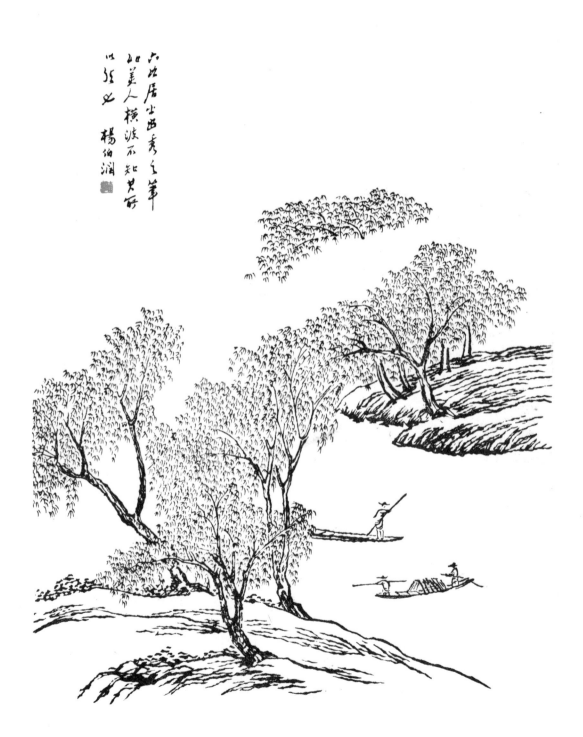

## A Clearing Sky

Wind sweeps the sky; it is like a mirror.
A day of broken clouds like blossoming duckweed.
Garden flowers are still wet;
Vegetable rinds are already green-tinted.
Powder on butterfly wings must be thinning out;
Ripples in ponds and marshes are becoming stagnant.
When I seek for spring, grudge me not inebriety;
Do not laugh because my hairs are few.

## GOING UP TO K'AN-SHAN PAVILION AFTER SNOW: WRITTEN IN HARMONY WITH SHIH-LANG[1] TZU-CHENG'S COMPOSITION

Blue fog on the lake, the freeze is not yet over;
Beautiful view of the lake might delay you.
Standing by the lofty tree I gaze at the peaks.
Rays of snow-colored mist drift towards my wine.

## DISTANT HILLS

Thousands of ridges stab at the clouds;
One glance is not enough.
Frontal ranges and the distant peaks,
Purplish blue, deep and light.

## LOTUS POOL

Unafraid of the dashing rain on the pool,
Enamelled leaves conceal each other.
Colorful birds suddenly fly in alarm,
Their rush scatters the sunset glow on the ripples.

# FISH POOL

Fogbound pool, somewhat shallow,
A mirror of green jade without the flowering caltrops.
When the sun's rays reach below the waves,
You can see fish and shrimp in the limpid river.

# The Paddy Field

Shallow jade-green water is flat,
Green paddy shoots grow.
Luckily they know the taste of the guest from Ch'u.
White paddy-birds fly high and low.

## A FOREST LANE COVERED WITH MOSS

Summer rain makes the forest muddy;
Slanting sunbeams reflect again and again.
Pure green, no wind ruffles it;
Let the spring grass smile!

# FARMERS LIVING BY THE RIVER

Slanting sunbeams divide the dawn on river,
They shine below the mulberry and *che* trees.[1]
On the high bank by the marsh sprouts of wheat grow;
They are green and can barely stand.
In the distance I see cows and sheep returning.
Affectionate youth was once carefree.
A drunken melody rises from the autumn grass;
I would rather live alone with this old family.

## PASSING WILD GEESE ISLET

Boat sails north from Wild Geese Islet;
Wild geese return bearing the spring breeze.
I only see flat sand and green water;
Tender shoots of thistle and artemisia are fattening side by side.

SEARCHING FOR THE MONK HUAI-HSIEN IN THE
YIN-CHING HILLS BUT NOT MEETING HIM

Delicate tendrils hang low from the pines;
Rush roots drink the jade-green spring.
The monk came not forth to meet us;
Sadly we return by the five high peaks.

## I STAY HOME ON AN AUTUMN DAY

Restless on my couch, I love the brightness of the blue sky;
Suddenly the worries of the world appear very small.
Hanging insects are swinging low from above;
Fighting sparrows fall to the ground but at once take off.
Now is the time to enter the cool bamboo grove,
And put off studies till tonight.
No man senses this calm landscape;
Moss color is reflected on my dress.

# VIEWING THE WILDERNESS

Fresh blue sky; this is the proper time to view the wilds.
I like most the mountain face.
Far and near, flowers mingle with bamboos;
High and low, water laps the fields.
Countless well-known birds call,
Inquire the name and age of the guest.
Here spring ploughing is late;
The lowing cow rests under the tree.

## FOR FU-KUO

Few peach trees have blossomed between the bamboos;
Spring moss grows in the lane to the Juan family home.
We open the door, call the horse and escort the departing guests;
Suddenly I feel the green and red dazzle my eyes.

## SNOW ON THE FIFTH DAY OF THE SECOND MONTH

Second month's raging wind and snow,
The freezing dawn is too severe.
I keep a vigil by the palace gate for my jealous lady;
Trees in the park add flowers unseen.
Dreams are full of butterflies;[1]
The long robe meets the hemp cloth.
I heave a cold sigh for my provider;
We meet and gamble till the rosy sunrise.

## The Yi Valley

Mountain gorge—the Yi flows.
The sound of current on the rocky bed
Seems more anxious at dawn and dusk.
The east ferry is about to leave;
People on the west dam are already standing.
Daily I watch the boat crossing east and west.
Rushing down this road I am too late.
Who can see the boy fishing
Wet and cold under a leafy cloak in this rain?

秋山蕾寺
仿祥明李
楊伯潤

Ou-yang Hsiu

## CLIMBING THE MOUNTAIN

Rapidly I climbed the high mountain,
Then sought out a steep ledge; I longed to enjoy this alone.
The fragrant grass by the rill was alarmed at first,
Suddenly I came across a hut overlooking the cliff.
The road by the forest edge I have lost already;
I can only follow the echo of the woodcutter's song.

## COMING DOWN THE MOUNTAIN

Walking and singing midst the subtle blue,
Together we descend the path ahead.
A thousand peaks glow in the setting sun,
A bird plunges downward from the cliff.
There is no one to man the evening ferry,
The boat is tied to a tree on the islet.

# ASCENDING THE SQUARE PAVILION

I hear the sound of bells floating across the cold water;
Step by step, together we climb to seek the cloudy peaks.
Following the solitary bird below us,
We look up towards the tiers of forests above.
You can still hear the sound of sutras from afar,
Sunset echoes amidst the empty hills.

## BOATING ON THE YI RIVER

The current gradually flows through the spring gorge,
Rippling eddies turn the small boat.
Sand birds shun human beings,
They fly towards the top of the green forest.

## RETURNING TO KUANG-HUA MONASTERY FROM P'U-T'I IN THE MOONLIGHT

Waterfall echoes amidst spring cliff,
Night is deep, mountain is already quiet.
Bright moon washes the pine forest,
All the peaks are the same tint.

## STONE-SCREEN[1] ROAD

The stone-screen lies beyond the floating clouds,
For long the stony path has known no human footprints.
I bring wine and get drunk below the screen;
Lying there I watch the autumn moon brightening all the peaks.

## After rain I walk alone on the north bank of the Lo River[1]

From the northern city tower I look towards the southern hills;
Shining mist mixed with purple fog.
Returning clouds move towards the Sung range,[2]
A shower passes over the Yi River.[3]
Trees surround the grassy bank;
The bridge lies athwart the glow of setting sun.
Lush greenery has made the imperial park half wild;
Wherever you stroll you hear only the cicadas.

# DISTANT HILLS

Mountain hues know no far or near,
Watching the mountains I could walk the whole day.
Peaks change from place to place,
I meet travellers, I know not their names.

## THREE POEMS WRITTEN ON A SPRING
## EXCURSION TO FENG-LO PAVILION

### I

Green trees crowd together and mountain birds sing,
Pure breeze ripples and falling flowers fly.
Song of bird, dance of flowers; I am drunk.
Tomorrow when I rise from my intoxicated slumber,
Spring will have gone already.

### II

Pale spring clouds and a bright sun,
Grass teases my robe as I walk;
Catkins brush against me.
Strolling up to the west of the pavilion you will meet me
Returning drunk in my bamboo sedan to transplant a flower.

### III

Red trees and green hills, sun is going down;
Green of grass dyes this vast open space.
Travellers care not for the aging spring,
In front of the pavilion they come and go,
Trampling the falling flowers.

## An informal drinking party with fellow prefects at the recently opened south annex of Huai Sung Pavilion[1]

Winding city walls are encircled with layers of mist and cloud;
Long ago someone here was sad, remembering the Sung mountains.
Mountains suddenly emerge when leaves of the frozen forest fall,
When the wild mums blossom, the wine matures.
West wind loosens my belt and rattles the hanging painting's corners,
I lean on the railings; the setting sun shines on blue pines.
In a drunken mood I meet my honored guest;
Treading on snow we view the jade-like peaks.

# PEASANT'S COTTAGE

Green mulberries shine all over the flat valley,
T'ien-shen[1] worship ends in laughter and shouts.
Beyond the forest doves coo and spring rain is over,
Early sun catches the gorgeous apricot flowers on the roof-top.

WHEN I FIRST CAME TO WEST LAKE AT YING-CHOU,[1] I PLANTED
LOTUS AND YELLOW POPLARS AND SENT THIS POEM TO HUAI-NAN[2]
FOR OFFICERS LÜ TU-CHIH AND HSÜ CHU-K'O

The vast flat lake is like green glazed glass,
Limpid shadows of its four sides have just met.
Willow catkins are no longer here; spring is far advanced.
The cherry-apple tree hates to see me arrive so late.
Chirruping birds seem to talk with travellers,
Bright moon lazily pulls, and the tiny boat follows.
When I reach these wonderful areas of rest,
I think of you and wish we were draining goblets together.

## THE YI-YÜAN BRIDGE

Red railings brighten the green water,
Ancient willows reflect the setting sun.
Where can one go to see this wonderful sight?
The Ch'ing-lien pavilion looks like a pair of girls.

# On the Way to Receive Imperial Orders

Rising sun warms with an auspicious glow.
I present myself at the Imperial Court in the capital.
I receive the ambassador's plaque in person.
By sunrise I have come out of the Ta-ming Palace;
Blue smoke rises from the Imperial capital;
Towers and terraces are in a white mist.
Embroidered saddle appears brilliant and proud,
One dimly sees the purple sable sleeves.
Whirlwinds in the northern lands are terrible;
Corners of the picture rollers[1] in the frontier city are thick and strong.
Passing over the bridge on the river, I cross the frontier;
I turn my head and admire those south-flying swans.
Here the land is crisscrossed with mountains and streams;
In the sky the same sun and moon remain.
Here children can ride horses,
Women carry bows in their girdles.
Traversing treacherous paths I am afraid of being lost;
On high mountains twisted paths seem to end.
I listen to the stags calling in the mountainous depths;
The wind rises from the dark forests.

Cold currents sound louder amidst the pines,
Icy rivulets choke, then flow again.
Viewing the plains I wonder how far the inn is;
In this vast wilderness the sky appears so immense.
Fine horses come from north of the mountains;
Swift hunting falcons come from the eastern seas.
After the hunt, birds and animals are gone;
The tent is shifted, the poolside left vacant.
When we honor faith, neighbors become friends;
When we respect virtue, ceremonies flourish.
We drink red wine with crushed ice;
And frozen meat with frosty red marks.
Grass stays white through the entire spring,
The whole day the sun is misty through the yellow sands.
New year comes and the wind changes;
On my way back the snows will melt early.
For this work one must have strength;
Alas! I am a sick old man.
I feel shame to compare myself with Su Wu,[1]
Who after his return never mentioned his own merits.

# A poem sent to the Pao-hsi Temple at Sha-ch'i[1]

I love Kiangsi, everything is so beautiful here.
I write poems praising these things for the northerners.
Frosty sun of the green forest dyes the maple leaves;
Autumn wind over the whitened water blows through paddy flowers.
Brew the wine, boil the chicken, detain the drunken guest;
Mountain cottages echo with looms weaving hemp.
The rustic priest alone secures immortal joy;
Sitting with his legs crossed, burns incense the whole day.

CLIMBING THE CENTER PEAK OF T'AI-SHIH MOUNTAIN[1]
STARTING FROM THE MIDDLE HALL OF CHÜN-CHI MONASTERY

I tether my horse in the shadow of green pines;
In my straw sandals I walk along the green cliff.
Startled birds stir the forest flowers;
Empty hills echo the human voice.
Glow of clouds penetrating the dark mist
Is beyond my power to capture.

## CHÜN-CHI MONASTERY

Enter the path and view the stone gate,
A vague green amidst the deep cloudy sky.
Clouds appear between the smooth stone steps,
Old trees and cold heavenly breeze.
Guests come to look at the last sun-glow,
And then hesitantly listen to the mountain cicadas.

## The Middle Peak

You look but cannot reach,
You walk, the road goes twisting.
A path appears on the wood top;
A thousand cliffs are visible beneath the clouds.
Fog and mist gleamed, now it is dark again.
The last glow lingers on the peak's tip.

# ANCHORING FOR THE NIGHT AT YÜEH-YANG[1]

Resting, I listen to the bells of Yüeh-yang town;
My boat is tied to a tree below the city wall.
I face the empty vast river; the moon rises;
In the intermingling of clouds and water the route is lost.
In the deep night the river moon displays clear light;
People return to the river to sing beneath the moon.
I could not hear the end of one drawn-out note;
A light boat with short paddles passed as if flying.

# Writing at the "Pavilion of the Drunken Old Man" at Ch'u-chou[1]

"Forty is not really old,"
The drunken old man suddenly writes on paper.
There is intoxication in many things;
How can I remember my years?
I love that patch of water below the pavilion
Where it trickles from the scattered mountains.
Sound of something falling from the sky:
Accumulated rainwater leaking through the front eaves;
It flows through the cliff and joins the stream below,
It bubbles in the darkened springs.
Its echo does not disturb our conversation;
Its pure sound shames flutes and strings.
How it dulls the sound of our instruments!
How it excels our guitars and flutes!
Let me lift my cup again and again;
The distant footfalls are the murmuring current.
Wild birds watch me in my intoxication,
Mountain clouds lull me to sleep.
Mountain flowers smile in seclusion;
I cannot describe it with my speech.
Only the wind from the cliff comes down
To breathe me into consciousness.

## The sky clears after a snowfall

The wild water comes gliding;
Glorious this spread of the West River.
Sun at dawn wraps itself in last night's clouds,
Desolate terrace reflects unmelted snow.
The view alters by the end of winter;
The calendar says this is a new month of the year.
Frozen plants have just burgeoned,
Green froth emerges and frolics in the water.
Men at leisure enjoy their friends,
Birds sing and you know the season.
We not only search for fragrant plants
But also inspect the mulberry farms.

# Western Garden

Dipping sun knocks at the rivulet gate;
Whence does the West River return?
People move in and plough amidst the trees,
Flowers fall when it rains in the fields.
Wilderness is level here, southern range is there.
Lonely terrace rises out of the wintry fog.
For whom does the music speak?
A man today still cherishes the past.

## On an evening stroll in the Lü-yin Park I go up the Ning-ts'ui Pavilion steps

The remnant of spring is far gone,
Green water overflows the new pool.
Love for the dense forest shadows is aroused in us;
First whiff of cool orchid breeze.
On the high terrace I can see on all sides;
Endless long green hills surround the city.
Wilderness tints improve in the evening,
Misty sunset is subtle and vague.
Lonely longings cannot be set down,
Alone I sing: With whom shall I toast the wine?
Bright moon seems to comfort me,
Open the alcove and let in the pure light.

# On the Tower

Over the hundred-foot-high tower
Ten thousand mountains fold.
I gaze south of the Ch'u River;[1]
Horizon is half clear, half misty.
Clouds hide the empty path;
It is nearly evening.
The curtain rolls up on twilight,
Moon is in the first quarter.
Mulberries drop in the town of P'u,[2]
Wine matures quickly.
Willows decay on the Chang terrace,
Feel the passed years.
My hair catches the light like a bush,
I restrain my sorrow.
Do not wait for youth, for it passes
Like a gust of wind.

## An Evening View at Ho-lung Men Pass

Vaporous mists drizzle; I look straight ahead;
Unhurried, I urge on my horse, humming a tune.
Smoke and mist are now bright, now dark;
There is a glow on the river.
In these empty and scattered mountains
Hundreds of birds are startled.

## A SOLITARY WALK BY THE YI RIVER[1]

Green trees wind around the Yi River,
People stroll among the scattered rocks.
Cold clouds lean on the waning sun,
White birds fly towards the blue hills.
Path turns; there is the Hsiang-lin monastery;
Since the monk is back the ferry stays idle.
Who can climb that sheer cliff?
With spent passion, I return empty once more.

AFTER THE SKY CLEARS, I GO TO SEE THE SNOW.
I WRITE THESE TWO POEMS AND PRESENT THEM
TO YÜAN CHEN, THE P'AN-KUAN[1]


I

Cold mountain over the river
Faces my doors.
Wild flowers and rock grass
Grow together on the rugged cliff.
Alone I hum a tune and view the jade-like peaks.
Idly I remember the person below the red-lotus curtain.


II

A superb view and no one by my side to see and toast it!
I end my day all alone, leaning on the tower railing.
The year comes to an end here in this mountain city;
I regret the passing of time.
The spring breeze makes me shiver.

## Two poems on Pai-hua Isle,[1] following the rhyme pattern of Sheng Yü's poems

### I

Wild banks, the stream curves a few times,
The pine path passes through a blue shadow.
I know not how far is the flowery islet,
But I love the deep green of this water-lily.

### II

Water-lily deep and luxuriant,
Water is deep and wind is strong.
Rain is over, a pure fragrance spreads.
Sunset tips the city tower,
Returning oar is followed by the shining moon.

# KUEI-YEN PAVILION AT HUA-CHOU

This long river, years end, many winds of sorrow have blown;
The pavilion with its old and derelict terrace half leans over the void.
Only when the wild geese return very early
Will the willows put forth tiny green specks
And the apricots be slightly tinged with red.

A BOAT TRIP ON WEST LAKE. A POEM DEDICATED TO
HIS EXCELLENCY THE YÜN-SHIH[1] AND ACADEMICIAN CHANG SHAN

Color of willows reflects on the waves with a dark green;
The decorated boat passes the winding islets and slanting bridges.
Still far more beautiful!—I am afraid all will end.
The water slowly deepens, the trees slowly grow denser and unending.
In silky fragrance the charming guests are detained,
Music comes soaring on the evening breeze.
We are half drunk and our boat lost direction on the way back;
Pavilions and towers rise tall against the evening sun.

# THE ANGLER

Wind pulls at the angler's line,
Curling gracefully along the rod.
A flat hat and a light cloak of leaves,
Amidst the sparse grass.
Spring rain drizzles;
He is faintly visible.
Mist has buried the hills ahead.

## LOTUS LEAVES

Wind comes over the pool and waves overflow;
They reveal layers of leaves.
Who opened these green parasols over the water?
Covering the crimson make-up,
Singing as they pick lotus.

## An early summer on West Lake

Heavy rain has come and gone,
A new blue appears, and the green stream overflows.
Casually I walk out alone,
Seeking this fresh greenness.
Dark green and golden orioles;
Spring has already passed.
Red flowers and green moss,
People rarely come.
Duckweed surrounds the islet,
Fishes jump about.
The days are long,
Swallows fly to and fro over the railings.
Monks roaming these woods care not for welcomes or farewells.
I like to sit on that catch-fish-stone facing the terrace.

# Su Shun-ch'in

# CHIN-SHAN MONASTERY

A solitary peak rises from out of the vast river,
Lofty halls are piled up on it.
Dangerous waves rise on all sides,
Day and night you hear the claps of thunder.
Dark ravine preserves wind and clouds,
On the south slope houses glimmer in green and gold.
Scattered red-berry trees,
Their roots enfolding the ancient stones.
Deep corridors surround the high halls,
Very attractive they look on the spine of the hill.
Images of departed friends float on the sea;
A cold light drips from the pearls and gems.
Sea-turtles and water-lizards are painted on the screen;
As I raise my head I am at peace.
Ups and downs come one after another,
But today I am satisfied with what I have received.
Those blue-winged birds are still there,
Flying around to delight the guests.
Holding violet flowers in their beaks,
They approach as if they know me.
I open my heart to this boundless space;
Above and below there is nothing strange.
Here there is a special quality,
Whatever you gaze upon is always delightful.
My spirit was noble and pure,
Falsely separated by earthly dust.
This earth was to me unknown,
I did not know such a spot could exist!
As the sun sets I shall get in my boat,
My head bowed in empty self-pity.

ANCHORED IN THE MIDDLE OF THE LAKE, IN COMPANY WITH CLOSE
FRIENDS, I COMPOSED THIS POEM AND PRESENTED IT TO CAPTAIN
HUANG ON THE NIGHT OF THE FIFTH DAY OF THE NINTH MONTH

I see a golden hook on a violet screen;
So many precious pearls remain motionless.
Bright and beautiful shadows shake on the waves,
A sandbar lies visible in the distance.
Hills ahead slowly darken, fisherman's song ceases,
A handful of reeds sigh for the end of autumn.
I stop rowing and gaze upon this view;
In times like this I think of travelling to the Great Walls.
Ch'ing-o[1] comes rowing across this vast space,
Suddenly she stops at a distance.
Though we have engaged her many times,
She still knits her brow in shame.
The four windows of her brightly painted boat are open;
Fragrant wine and tasty morsels[2] are to entertain guests.
The song ends, but its crystal echo lingers,
Laughter moves the gay beauty, perfume rises from her silk dress.
Jade platter and the minced perch gleam alike,
Bamboo-shoots and fruit kernels are set out for our pleasure.
The Milky Way slants across the sky,
Orion turns over.
Atmosphere in the boat becomes congenial;
I rise to drink your health, you pledge me with wine.
We both know this is a rare gathering,
This unexpected meeting will be rarer in the future.
Only now do I realize that I work as a menial;
There is so much sadness for us all on this disturbed earth.
No sooner drunk than we ask for more songs and dances.
Tomorrow all this will scatter in the void,
Leaving only the melancholy.

## Sky clears on a spring evening

People say spring rains are good,
Even better if evening comes fair and clear.
Trees turn green through the curtain,
A touch of fog makes all things bright.
Early swallows are happy for the mud;[1]
Like a released arrow fly the wild swans.
Who looks out from the lofty tower?
The setting sun is at the far horizon.

## Journeying Alone to Wang-ch'uan[1]

Walking through blue clouds;
Mountain torrents inaccessible,
Drop with faint sounds of bells.
A few furlongs I walk over loose stones,
A stream encircles the blue mountain peak.
In the dark forests tailed-deer let their horns grow,
Tigers leave pawprints on the paths.
Have you perchance met the hermit
Sighing alone facing the ancient pine?

## Composing at the Residence of Senior Official Li at Fan-ch'uan[1]

East of T'u-chü[2] the scenery is wonderful;
I arrive, tether my horse, stay alone a long time.
Blue shadow of countless mountains in front of the gate,
The cold sound of rushing water below the bamboos.
The wine is covered with a new layer of dust;
Frequently I get drunk.
Flowers bloom and I know not how many autumns have passed;
My host's table is heaped with official work.
He returns to it morning and evening,
And now there is a touch of white in his hair.

## Evening sky clears over the Hsin-k'ai Lake

Rosy clouds are lost in the east and west,
Water moves in the sky amidst this glittering void.
The numerous tiny boats are like wandering birds,
Riding the wind in an empty sky.

# At the reception pavilion, south of the city of Yang-chou[1]

Confused humming of cicadas,
Willows in a faint mist.
Alone on the lofty tower,
I look down at the radiance of the setting sun.
I see the mountains across the river,
The forest below.
City folks head towards the ferry;
Wind and smoke from far and near
Are about to lift.
It is difficult to appease the perverse power
Of wolf and tiger.
Let them come out and take charge.
It is useless for me to make trouble for myself;
Alas! I wish I knew what course to follow!

# Tseng Kung

江山帆影
耕烟用董
蒼古秀
潤沙宋人
法
尚湖伯潤

# SONG OF SNOW

Huge blocks of ice choke streams and marshes,
Noisy north wind cries around trees and stones.
A thousand miles of yellow clouds at midnight,
By early dawn the snow is a foot deep.
There is a delicate balance between yang and yin;
Many species leave no footprints in the dust.
The flood dragon rises to embrace lofty mountain peaks;
Waters running crosswise obstruct the lanes and roads.
The wild misty forest takes the shape of doom,
Trees in the courtyard look new and beautiful,
But I doubt if one can pluck the leaves.
Open the door and sense the silent mountain village;
Scattered books lean against the white papered windows.
Bright light shines all over this mountain valley,
Vision is clear; see those lofty firs and cedars.
Young men raise their eyes and look at the tower,
The strong man aspires only to confront the desert.
Hungry squirrels crying, hiding their teeth and claws in winter sleep,
Hunting hawks circle to catch anything on wings.
Under thatched eaves guests gather round elegant wine jars,
People walk the mulberry lane sinking in their wooden shoes.
The high palace is comfortably warm and summer silks are in style.
Below the wall the poor are clad in coarse linen.
How can one bear to look out at the white sunshine?
Sitting here I can see the edge of the sand.
Gradually the sunken ditch foretells good harvest,
Flowing water washes the village street of epidemics.
Seize the opportunity of the rising northeaster;
Drive the exhausted cow and burn the unfertile hilltops.

## ROAMING THE LANG-YEH MOUNTAINS[1]

Darting rays melt the piles of snow,
Southern mountains expose their rocky heights.
Waters of Yangtze and Huai are not yet green,
Deep valley flowers have already blossomed.
From afar I hear the sound of the mountain spring,
Muffled sound like the breaking of ice in a ravine.
Who once loved those greens and blues?
Those piled up hanging towers and terraces?
Tier after tier of beams and poles,
Shining like engraved jasper.
Though you have the quality of a phoenix,
You cannot avoid the envy of swallows and sparrows.
The cry of displaced birds
Flying round and round this mountain bend.
All things that make up the human body,
Even this world is but a speck of dust.
I only want to clasp truth and virtue;
I am not ashamed to follow Ch'iu and Hui.[2]
One follows where these masters lead;
Who can foresee the shore or the precipice?
Who can write down all my thoughts,
All that happened in joy and laughter?
I speak with those who work under me,
And drink my fill of this delicious country spirit.

## Peach Blossom Spring

I come in autumn and there are no peach blossoms;
Bare trees, and a cold spring spills over the stony bank.
When they fight, men look for pomp and glory,
They never learn to love mountains and rivers.

# The Pan-shan Pavilion[1]

Tree tips are green, cliff path crouches and coils;
At late noon this half-way pavilion is still cold.
Ordinarily you should look up and view the mountain;
Reaching here, I lean on the balustrade and look straight down.

## CHAO-YIN MONASTERY

A narrow lane enters the pines,
Two peaks lie facing my horse.
Struggle up this green wistaria-covered ledge,
Reach the azure cliff top with running steps.
Recluses hid here in the past,
Fingers played music over red silken strings.
Meditate over the moon between the pines;
Alone you paint a fountain in the mountain.
This joy is your own, not for others to share.
Why should I tug the net of worldly attachments?
I have always been a man of quiet leisure;
Arriving here I feel more happiness.
I am overfond of lonely places
Where water flows and sings.

## Bright Weather After a Snowfall: Sixth Day of the First Month

Melted snow of mountain torrents is full of spirit,
My eyes are filled with east wind.
This augurs an early spring.
Tomorrow the apricot garden should be ablaze;
It is time to make an appointment to see my flower girl.

# PAVILION ON THE CH'IAO-SHAN[1]

The great pavilion rises, pressing close to the city heights;
Its lofty corners stab at the purple mist.
Stern of a boat comes floating
Along the wild bank of the Lo River.
Magpie Mountain towers black,
Piercing the pure sky.
Who can equal Shao Ling's poetry now,[2]
While the style of Tung-hai school spreads the world over?
The prefect[3] hums and laughs at himself;
It is time to go back.
I hesitate under the ascending moon.

## ENJOYING THE COOL BREEZE AT WEST LAKE

If you ask me where one can avoid this blazing heat,
The vast expanse of West Lake lies before your eyes.
Fishes play round a reed, fresh waves come in full;
Birds twitter and there is a green shadow everywhere,
A rainbow is dimly visible over the pine bridge,
A hawk's head painted high on the moving boat.
I deeply enjoy a cool evening breeze and a lovely moon;
Amid the perfume of purple lotuses
I listen to the sound of a bubbling spring.

# CITY TOWER

The higher I go up the tower the more my eyes are filled with mountains.
It was an accident that this idler came here to roam.
As the wind rises, snow flies endlessly;
Wild water carries the rain knowing no bounds.
Thinking of old things and old friends,
One has the feelings of a returning swallow.
To be at peace and harmony is more like a seagull.
Teams of horses with gold trappings will come to dust;
Don't be stingy, enjoy yourself with a hundred bowls of wine.

## POEMS WRITTEN AFTER LEAVING CH'I-CHOU[1]

### I

Cloud sails, ten in number, move with the wind;
Reclining, I listen to the sound of white ripples that follow my boat.
The wonderful sight of the rising moon over the breaking waves of West Lake.
Waking from a drunken sleep, I still look at the brightening papered window.

### II

This whole day my pleasure-boat has crawled midst the sand bars;
It is already a month since I left Ch'i-chou.
For all these many miles the one who has followed me is the bright moon.
By the west pavilion a boat brightens the water.

### III

Bark of trees has put on a sharp, bright design;
Dark blue spots on the fields have blossomed with water lilies.
Now is the time to go to the west pavilion to escape the summer days;
But can you forget sorrow by living amidst mists and waves?

### V

Perfume of lotus cools my pillow and mat,
Sound of water intoxicated with autumn penetrates the curtains.
Looking around this vast expanse, only a single sail within a thousand miles,
A quiet boat, and I am all alone by the window.

# TOWER AT KAN-LU MONASTERY

If you wish to absorb the beautiful views from this tower,
Then lazily recline on these railings and gaze around.
Confused clouds and glittering water drifting away in blue and purple,
Mountain mists reaching the sky in varied hues.
The bell intones "Moon, south of Huai river,"
From afar comes the ocean wind to catch our sails.
Though I am old, the dust of the world clings to my robe;
I wish only to admire the high-flying geese.

# A Trip to the Suburbs

The bean leaves hurry us to plough,
It is the second month.
The inclined bridge and the winding shoreline,
My horse ambles along.
Every family is selling wine,
Ch'ing-ming festival[1] is near
Red and white flowers have blossomed on a branch or two.

# The West Tower

Clouds like sea waves come and go,
Blowing north wind raises a few rumblings of thunder.
Fine bamboo screens hang on four sides of the tower;
Reclining, I watch the rush of rain over a thousand hills.

## TWO POEMS WRITTEN WHILE I WAS AT THE SOUTH OF THE CAPITAL

### I

Rains drove across the pool, the dike is filled with water;
Over these scattered hills roads wind east and west.
The first blossoms of peaches and plums are exhausted,
Now there is only green grass to compete for colors.

### II

Long pool is filled with water, the rains have passed;
A confused shadowy red is flying everywhere.
Seeing spring go out, I feel intense loss,
I will roam afar but may never return here.

# Ssu-ma Kuang

意念愈簡而愈多態愈
老而愈媚　楊伯潤

## TOWER OF A COUNTY TOWN

A solitary tower,
Not very high,
But high enough to give a view.
Farm women are returning on the road
After feeding their menfolk in the field.
Farmers have their meals in the shade of the mulberries.
I instruct the officers to reduce taxes;
It won't do to let farming suffer.

# WILLOWS

Highroads are clogged with carts and horses;
Farmlands suffer from the officials' axe.
Who planted these trees opposite the magistrate's residence?
I am old and useless but pure in spirit.
Sir, what I wish is a heart like yours,
Preserving trees is like preserving human life.

# Wang An-shih

## On an Occasion

A cloud rises from the Chung-shan range,[1]
Yet it enters Chung-shan.
May I inquire of the mountain folks,
Where is that cloud now?

# THE T'AI-PAI RANGE[1]

Steep and lofty, the T'ai-pai runs southeast,
Other ranges encircle it in blue confusion.
Mists and clouds, thick or thin, are all so lovely;
Trees and rocks, far and near, are all in harmony.
Bright spring is here and birds chatter joyfully,
Mountain brook is stilled and fish move slowly.
Where can I find a place like this to live
So that I can share the joy of fishes and birds?

# A SPRING EVENING ON PAN-SHAN MOUNTAIN[1]

The spring breeze carried the flowers away;
Rewards me with a pure *yin* feeling.[2]
This screened sloping road is quiet,
Adjoining bower is hidden in depth.
I arrange my bed and rest awhile;
With a staff and straw sandals
I roam for a lonely search.
Only the birds of northern mountains are passing through,
Leaving behind a lovely tune.

# On the road to Tung-yang[1]

Mountains that hide the sky of Wu[2] are dense;
River that coils in the land of Ch'u[3] is deep.
Here the drifting clouds mass like white jade,
The setting sun pours yellow gold.
Boundless, they follow as I travel;
The seasons come and go.
I urge myself to sing about these things,
And ready myself to help the world.

## Entering the North Monastery in Pai-t'u Village

Farmers' cottages appear over the treetops,
North of the town is crisscrossed with rustic lanes.
Canal flows in dark green jade,
Farm plots rest against yellow clouds.
Fading hibiscus is dipped in rouge,
Deep water full of lotus smells of musk.
A setting sun, and no one is about,
Chickens and ducks are keeping company.

# IN THE HUI-CHÜ MONASTERY ON THE K'UN SHAN MOUNTAINS
## (MODELED ON CHANG HU'S RHYME)

Mountain peaks appear and disappear;
Rivers and lakes flow and ebb.
Gardens and groves seem to float at the cape;
Towers and temples crowd the crest of the hill.
For a hundred miles I see the fishing boats;
A thousand families hide in that village by the coast.
Land ends here; travellers come rarely.
The company of monks gives me a melancholy joy.

## TOURING THE SHENG-KUO MONASTERY IN HANGCHOW

I view the landscape as I go up;
I am in the midst of water.
Below the towers,
Nothing but the green of trees.
Floating clouds meet the ocean breeze,
Setting sun vibrates its light on the lake.
For once I sit and play my flute;
This faint melody enters Fuyang.[1]

## SPRING BREEZE

A gust of spring breeze; swallows are heading north.
I imagine myself again in the midst of old hills and rivers.
Sunlight reflects on the river by the edge of the wood;
Dust eddies upwards from the plains,
Smoke of a prairie fire rises.
The sun lends a delicate yellow to the willow tips,
The rain quickens the new green that returns to the fields.
As I look back I fail to notice the flowering magnolia;
I realize that I saw those flowers a year ago.

## ON THE RIVER

The river ripples in the west wind,
Bubbles fade in the evening glow.
A fond farewell from my short flute;
I played on it east of these scattered hills.

## PAVILION AT THE WEST T'AI-YI KUNG PALACE

By the grass border blossoming lotuses shed their petals,
Willows and poplars droop by the water.
At sunset the solitary smoke from cooking rises;
I do not know which family owns this fishing net.

## Autumn Clouds

Autumn clouds release their rain on this quiet mountain forest;
Thousands of dikes break,
Water rushes in one united roar.
I wish to record this barren winter but cannot paint it;
To transmit my grief and my resolve, I play on my harp.

# TREETOPS

Treetops in the north mountains come gently out of fog;
Grass roots tinkle in the southern mountain torrents.
Silk turns white as snow when mulberry leaves are very green;
After the first harvest of yellow clouds,[1] rice plants are just freshening.

# WIND OF SPRING

The spring wind passes over the willows,
They are green like silk.
Blue sky and sun warms the red on tiny peaches.
Fishes come to the warm fragrant corner of the pool.
Amidst all this the pavilion by the river
Bursts like a bubble on limpid waves.

# Anchoring the boat at Melon Island

Water separates Ching-k'ou[1] from the Melon Isle;
A few folds of mountains away is the Chung-shan range.[2]
Spring breeze dyes the south bank green,
When will the bright moon shine on my return?

# On Chin-ling[1]

By the water my cottage door is ajar;
A little bridge,
A branch road enters the green moss,
Behind me the shadows of endless willow forest,
Fragrance coming from the next cottage is of plum flowers.

# North of the City

Robe of spring covers thousand miles of green fields,
Night rain hastens the red tint on the tiny peaches.
Immersed in thought, I turn my head towards the North City;
A bright sun and a clean valley with wild clouds on high.

# Looking at a Picture of Ming-chou Town[1]

Outer walls of Ming-chou are recorded in painting;
I remember the West Pavilion shaped like a boat.
Surrendering to bygone emotions, one cannot relive the past;
Even in those days the landscape remained as before.

# A Ballad of Chung Mountains[1]

Mountain stream silently curves round the bamboos;
West of the bamboos flowers and grass play with the spring's tenderness.
Under the eaves of the thatched roof we sit
Facing each other the whole day.
Not a single bird calls; the mountain grows more gloomy.

# On the River

North of the river autumn clouds are half open;
A hesitant rain comes down from the evening clouds.
Blue mountains wind around,
I suspect there are no roads.
Then suddenly I see a thousand glimmering sails approach.

## My Residence at Ting-lin[1]

The cottage goes round the curved creek;
Bamboos follow the bend of the mountain.
Streams and mountains are still there
In the midst of white clouds.
Come to the creek and free the skiff;
Sit here with your back to the mountain.
With the river birds and mountain flowers,
Share my leisure.

## Spring Day

Green moss shines on water by my cottage door;
Spring surrounds the slowly budding flowery branches.
This is a long road; travellers cannot come here.
It is a long day; birds twitter as they fly back and forth.

## Apricot Blossoms

A path with drooping willows,
Sealed with purple moss.
Murmur of voices within the compound,
Only apricot blossoms welcome guests.
A setting sun leans on the wall
Reddening several branches.

## A SKY JUST CLEARED OF CLOUDS

Touch of a rosy cloud amidst dark crimson;
Snowflakes begin to melt in the grooves of roof-tiles.
Mountains ahead have not set free their morning cold,
Yet a few peaks are locked in white clouds.

## On Departure from Chin-ling[1]

Dense grass and trees crest the White Stone Hill;
Spring breeze disarrays my robes.
Drifting clouds over the dazzling city mean good weather;
Men are followed by flying birds making wonderful music.

# Su Shih

# DRAGON TEMPLE

Evening ferry cuts across the jade-green river;
At night, on horseback I enter South Mountain valley.
Dark waters roar in the gorge;
Distant stars shine brightly on the mountain ranges.
A temple is hidden at the foot of the cliff, thousands of fathoms below.
Road twists round the mountain's waist: three hundred coils.
Wind rises; in the empty forest the hungry tiger roars.
Moon darkens, startled deer and squirrels run to distant bamboo groves.
Inside the door the empty altar, then the deep, vast temple;
Guttering candles illumine the Buddha in green.
Shameless travellers carry in wine and food,
Chop pinewood and boil vegetables in water from the mountain stream.
Guests sleeping on wooden planks are startled from their pillows;
At dawn wooden clappers announce the monks' gruel.
I look up and see thousands of tiles rising dense and uneven;
The eye is lost amid a thousand cliffs, scattering red and green.
Traders sell peppery tea at the gate; Szechwan is just over the mountains.
When shall I return to plough by the river?
All night long my heart was flying south with the snow-goose.

## Ta-ch'in Monastery[1]

The vast bright valley is flat;
Blue foothills slope across it.
A solitary pagoda appears far off;
All alone it faces the scattered shining hills.
Aimless I walk, seeking joy in far places;
Warning comes with the wind,
These level fields are like a sea,
With waves rolling eastwards.

COMPOSED ON THE WANG-HU PAVILION AFTER A CAROUSE
(27TH DAY OF THE SIXTH MONTH)


Black clouds pouring ink do not hide the hills;
White raindrops like bouncing pearls scatter inside the boat.
Wind comes rolling over the land to blow them away;
Below the Wang-hu Pavilion the water is like the sky.

## Evening scene from the Wang-hai Pavilion

Ocean waves come single file,
Instantly drift like snow in front of the pavilion.
Now you must ascend as the tide rises;
Twenty times more will you see those silvery mountainous waves.

## DRINKING ON THE LAKES AFTER THE SKY HAS CLEARED

Sparkling water rolls like the sea, clear sky is fine;
The mountain has a hazy look, the rain is wonderful.
I feel urged to compare the Western Lake with Hsi-tzu:[1]
Light make-up or heavy, she always remains a beauty.

## VILLAGE IN THE MOUNTAIN

Bamboo fence and thatched cottages lie across the stream,
Spring enters the mountain village, flowers everywhere.
Great peace, though formless, here finds its form;
Solitary smoke curls upward; men live there.

# On the road to Hsin-ch'eng

East wind knows I wish to go to the mountains;
It blows and stops the sound of ceaseless rain between the eaves.
Light clouds on the range wear a cotton-wool cap;
On the treetops the new sun hangs a copper gong.
Wild peaches smile, the bamboo fences are low;
Willows by the stream sway in pleasure, water in the sand is clear.
People who dwell in the Hsi-yen[1] mountains are the happiest;
Boil the celery, bake the tender bamboo shoots to serve the ploughman in the spring.

## Han-lu Creek

Shimmering bright creek ripples with a spring sparkle;
Time for tender shoots of reeds to grow, willow catkins fly.
No matter that the south wind still blows from across the river;
Peach flowers float on the water and the knife-fish grows fat.

## LI SZU-HSÜN PAINTS LONG RIVER
### WITH ITS BARREN ISLANDS

Green mountains and vast boundless river,
Lonely is the rock in the middle of the river.
Ruined path is dangerous, only birds and monkeys go there;
A bridge with a wooden support for the day-long traveller.
From whence comes the boat with singing oars?
In the wind that smooths the sand I hear them rising and falling in the current;
Little hope of staying in that lonely hill for long.
Over the boat jut two high peaks;
Misty-haired Dawn begins her new make-up in the mirror.
The merchant in the boat is not upset;
Last year he married his only daughter to a strong and handsome groom.

## Writing on the wall of Hsi-lin Monastery

With a sidelong glance I see the never-ending peaks lying crosswise;
Far and near, high and low, not one is the same.
I cannot even recognize Lu Mountain directly before my eyes,
Because my body is still in the mountains.

# Climbing Yün-lung Mountain[1]

Drunk, I walk along the Huang-mao[2] cliff;
The whole cliff is strewn with boulders like flocks of sheep.
I stumble to the edge of the cliff by the stone seat;
Looking up I see white clouds filling the sky.
The sound of songs falls into the ravine, the autumn wind blows sharply.
The men on the path lift their heads and look towards the southeast;
Boisterous Shih-chün[3] claps his hands and laughs loudly.

A SPRING RIVER AT DAWN:
A LANDSCAPE BY HUI TS'UNG[1]


Outside the bamboo grove are two or three branches of peach flowers;
River water is warm in spring, and the ducks know that first.
Artemisia carpets the ground;
Now is the time for the porpoise to rise.

## Resting in a Villager's Hut Twenty-five *li* South of the Shih-t'ien Posthouse on my Way to Yün from Hsing-kuo

Blue mountains in a hundred tiers over the mountain stream;
With a fast horse and light dress, I had a quick trip.
Bamboos and houses lean against the mountain;
The clear spring across the road knows I am thirsty.
Straw sandals and bamboo staff are light and comfortable;
The rush-mat and pine-needle bed are fragrant and smooth.
Midnight finds wind and dew covering the courtyard;
I see only a solitary glow-worm through the open door.

## Modeled on the rhymes of Ts'an Liao

Dawn comes, spreading a white rug;
Towers, pavilions, mountains and rivers—all look alike.
All are glittering silver, like white jade;
I do not know who is hoarding this rare work.

## Autumn mountains and fields: A painting by Kuo Hsi[1]

The Yü-t'ang hall screens the spring sun;
Within these walls is Kuo Hsi's painting of the spring mountains.
Cooing pigeons and young swallows are just awake from sleep;
The white waves and green peaks are not of this world.
The pair of short scrolls reveals the distant fields;
Distant forest looks wonderful this autumn evening.
As in those days south of the Yangtze River when, accompanying my guests,
I looked back from the middle of the stream and saw the clouds and peaks.
The Yi River[2] is old, with white frost at its temples;
Lying in bed I see the autumn hills and think of Lo-yang.[3]
The prince added his quick calligraphy at the end of the roll,
As clear as the great Lo,[4] drifting in the autumn glow.
I am free from public duty just for a day,
But my grey hair cannot reflect the green hills.
To paint Lungmen[5] with sandbanks,
We must wait till the Yi River buys off the mountain springs.

## Li Shih-nan paints autumn landscapes

### I

Wild trees in confusion descend towards the high-tide mark;
The distant forest, verdant green, has frost around its roots.
From whence comes the boat with the single oar?
My home is south of the Yangtze, in Huang-yeh village.

### II

In this world, sharp weapons daily make us behave like the barbarians.
Who takes time to see the beauty of the hundred-foot coils of dragons and snakes?
Was it you who travelled alone amid those mountains and rivulets?
Who else could create that ape hanging by his toes?

## MORNING BREAKS OVER THE HUAI RIVER

The pale moon drives the clouds towards the dawn;
A slight breeze blows across the water, ruffling the fishes' green scales.
Now I have decided to grow old with these rivers and lakes;
Silently I count ten waves coming from the middle of the Huai.

# KIANGSI

Kiangsi is my country.
White sand, green-blue bamboos, and pebbled riverbeds.
The boat travels ten *li* through nine whirling rapids;
The punting pole pounds against rocks like a mortar.
I lie down drunk and wake to the sound of running water;
Like old P'ang I wish to suck a mouthful of this water.
How expert the man watching for fish from the stone bridge!
With a loud cry he spears a pair of carp with his fork.

寒林霽雪
擬李營邱
南潮外史
楊伯潤

春陰漠漠重
岭岭江上人家
早闭門仿佛
茫耶溪畔
駐小橋流水
生蓮村
楊伯潤

## HSIEN-SHENG MONASTERY

In that dim forest in the distance the evening crows have gathered;
Solitary smoke in the lonesome village rises from the Buddhist temple.
Hermits planted a thousand orange trees;
Guests from afar come to seek the hundred garlands.
Pumice stones are already dry in the frosty water;
I leisurely pour a cup of tea from the hearth and taste it before the rains start.
I only doubt my dream of returning from the southwest
To blue bamboos and the village wrapped in white sand.

# THE PI-LO GROTTO

Jagged peaks joined in disorder,
Light rays slant across the precipice.
In the distance, amid blue and purple,
From ancient times dwelt holy men.
The southern cliff is lighted by the morning sun,
Its height touches the Heavenly Capital.[1]
The northern ravine restrains the white moon;
In dream I visit the magic city.
If indeed the stone gates part,
Silver river will pour forth.
A silent shrine in the sombre depths,
Another door admits the blameless soul.
The fountain wears strings of pearls,
Stalactites hang like woven silken tassels.
I fear that others may know I am here;
An immortal may appear to welcome me.
Whispers raise loud echoes,
Empty mountains warn with thunders.
Staff in hand, I turn back;
To make this trip I troubled Fung-p'ing.[2]

## Plum blossoms in flower below the Pine Wind Pavilion: The 26th day of the Eleventh Month

In the Huai-nan village on the Spring Wind Range,
The plum blossoms on the ancient trees are ready to fade.
When will they return, now that they want to drift away?
Savage wind and heavy raindrops, a sad twilight;
Long branches of lichee trees half-drooping by the river;
Leaning palms look elegant in the grove.
Why do only the sombre rays hold the shades of night?
But alas, the cold beauty will thrust out the warmth of winter.
In the brambles below the Pine Wind Pavilion
Two passion-flowers will bloom tomorrow at sunrise.
The fairy clouds from south of the seas will fall with grace
Below the stony flight of steps.
The moon will arrive clad in white silk and come knocking at my door.
Waking from a wine-steeped dream my senses are enraptured by these trees;
A strange feeling, inexpressible.
Sir, don't heave a sigh at solitary drinking;
You're lucky: the setting moon peeps in your empty goblet.

## I WRITE ANOTHER POEM FOLLOWING THE RHYME OF THE LAST ONE

Plum-Blossom village nestles below the Lo-fou[1] hills;
Jade-white snow is the bones, and water the soul.
The hesitant moon hangs in the trees,
Bright and lonely, it shines in the dusk.
You live apart on rivers and seas;
Do you feel anxiety like the sick crane nesting in a wild garden?
Heaven is fragrant and the land beautiful;
It is possible to admire both.
I entertain myself with mellowed wine,
My poems are clear and full of warmth.
Fairy servants of the fairy palace,
Wearing green dresses all ruffled,
The mulberry trees support the rising sun.
It peeps, enfolding the trees, and I lie down drunk;
With reason, I banish the woodpecker for tapping on the door.
The village maiden passes and the gentlemen hastily sweep aside the remnants of
    the wine;
Birds sing and dance and flowers speak.
People rising from their drunken sleep disperse on the solitary mountain.
Only the fallen pistils remain in sticky and empty goblets.

## A visit to Hsiang-ch'i Monastery at Po-lo[1]
### (with a preface)

The monastery is seven *li* away from the district town. Jagged mountains and fertile fields press on the two sides of the road. Wheat grows in profusion. The stream below the monastery can be used for a watermill. If a hundred-steps-long dike and a water-gate to control the flood can be built, then it can operate two mills and four pestles. I spoke about this to Magistrate Lin and ordered him to supervise and complete the work.

> For two years I have wandered in the land of fishes and frogs;
> In the morning I delighted to see the ripened beards of wheat.
> Easterly wind sways and the pure green dances,
> Early sun glistens on the dew, a happy and graceful yellow.
> Expanse of spring mud, already knee deep;
> Fresh autumn grain separated in bundles.
> Who says the life of a traveller is friendless?
> When I saw all this beauty I was delirious with joy.
> Three hills embrace like a screen, the monk's house is small;
> A ravine where water rolls like thunder and pine shade is cool.
> I want to use this water power for grinding,
> Build a dike that traces the veins of earth.
> Then we shall see flour pouring like snow,
> The pounding of husks like distant drums.
> Scattered fragments of white clouds split into beautiful coral shapes.
> Not only must the cakes have traditional flavor,
> The Supreme One[2] must be dissolved in the immortal wine.
> On finishing the poem I am convulsed with laughter:
> When a scholar speaks of food he speaks of the unobtainable!

## ENDLESS RAIN FLOODS THE RIVER

### I

Over the Yüeh-ching Mountains[1] clouds arise,
Waters of Tsangko River, vast as the sky.
The recluse is in his hut;
How avoid the leaking roof over the wet bed?
The cottages of the Tan tribes look like boats by the river.
Snakes, fish and prawns come down with the rain;
People with their dogs and chickens sleep on the high walls.
The tower steps are submerged;
I always remember the year I made it over the mountain pass.

### II

This heavy rain is mournful, but it cools the evening;
In bed, I hear the noise of the banyan leaves in the avenue.
Faint lamplight lightens my shattered dream,
Half-wet curtains give out a moist old fragrance.
Hidden in my high bed I play the clay flute;
Beyond the closed door trees wave and tinkle like gems.
Sir, do not go out; fair weather will not come;
Leave those empty flights of steps. It will rain the whole night long.

# Two poems written on the 29th day of the Third Month

## I

Clouds pass over the south range, a purple blue appears;
Rains flying across the North River bring melancholy.
I woke from a drunken dream to this end-of-spring day;
I close my door, lean on the table, and burn incense.

## II

Orange blossoms outside my door are still bright;
Lichees on the wall are already spotted.
Where the trees look dark and grass is deep, it is quiet there;
I roll up the curtain, lean on my pillow, and view the mountain.

# T'ung-ch'ao Pavilion at Teng-mai-yi[1]

## I

The weary traveller is sad to hear of the long road home;
Glittering corners of the pavilion roof look down towards the long bridge.
I gaze with longing at the white heron across the autumn creek;
I was unaware that the green forest had merged in the evening damp.

## II

I wish to spend my few last days in a Hainan village;
The emperor will send Wu Yang[2] to call back my soul.
Below this sombre sky falcons have no place to fly;
That thin hairline of blue hills yonder is China.

## I CALL ON THE PRIEST OF LING-SHANG
### BUT DO NOT MEET HIM

Bright rays of red flowers fill the balustrade;
The green of the grass is boundless.
I failed to meet the blue-eyed monk;
But I sang loudly by the white stone rivulet.

## Passing through Yi-pin country[1] I gaze at scattered hills in the land of the barbarians

I do not know this cold clear river,
In the distance the sun is on the mountaintop.
The moon at dawn clings to the high peak;
A bright vast space projects across the steep hill screen.
Clouds blow across and suddenly disperse;
Blue trees grow everywhere.
Travellers bow to that solitary glow,
Birds fly towards distant clouds.
Who can remember this wilderness without love?
Who can pluck here the thick rich grain?
Can we not avoid worldly scholars
And refine ourselves with that mysterious essence?
Who can take this winding road?
It bears the paw-marks of jackals and tigers.

## LOOKING AT MOUNTAINS FROM THE RIVER

Watching mountains from a boat is like looking at moving horses;
In a moment they pass in droves of hundreds.
Jagged teeth of the mountain ahead suddenly change shape;
Ranges left behind are like a confused and alarmed pack.
Looking up I see the narrow path winding round and round;
Travellers are dimly seen near the top.
I raise my hands from the boat wishing to talk to them;
Lonely sail goes south like a flying bird.

# ENTERING THE YANGTZE GORGE

For long have I cherished the desire to enjoy the gloom;
Today I have freedom to explore.
The Yangtze joins the lands of Ch'u and Shu,[1]
A thousand branches flow south and east.
Ho River strikes like lightning,
Green waves of Ch'ien turn blue.
Other currents are far too many;
From afar they come rushing together.
Entering the gorge roads disappear;
Interlocked mountains are like a shrine.
Winding around they tower in this vast water,
Shrinking an abyss into a pool.
Wind sounds like breath, clouds rise like spittle.
Hanging cliffs whisper, dangling creepers are fresh and green.
Cliff bamboos look cold and blue, a lonesome stone-cedar grows.
Spray flies like tumbling snow, strange stones shaped like alarmed horses.
To cross these streams one must know their depth;
Some boys suddenly appear gathering wood for fuel.
By chance appear some human dwellings;
On the sand bank you can get a sedan chair.
By seven in the evening the region is deserted;
The local lord is an old-fashioned moralist.
The *yamen* closes its doors when the evening drum sounds.
Guests are entertained with frozen oranges.
I have heard that here grows the Huang-ching grass;
Green-jade bamboos flourish.
I eat and drink my fill
But no P'eng or Tan[2] appears.
Climate is mild here in winter,
Milky Way stays half submerged at night.
Old loyalists still mourn for Ch'ang and Yen;[3]
It is an old custom to accept fish and silkworms as gifts.
Houses are made of boards but use no tiles,
Hillside huts are narrow like monasteries.
To go out and cut firewood is an adventure here;
Never does one get a full pot of rice.
Pity, what a poor life!

They work hard and are not ashamed.
This leaf of a boat lightly travels far;
It is strong against big waves.
Terror melts away, we look at each other with a vacant stare;
They utter something but we cannot converse.
How can one live in such wild and barren lands?
It is difficult to take delight in this dark gloom.
I only like that lonely pigeon-hawk resting
A hundred feet above the mountain mist.
It flies across with great poise,
It flies far, seemingly without effort.
Wings flapping, it flies towards the Milky Way,
Caring not for sparrows or quails.
This is a sick world of dust and toil,
Restraints I face are unbearable.
To dwell in complete retirement like a recluse,
How wonderful that would be!
But we are all drunk with worldly desires.
I watch the joy of a flying bird,
Hiding my desires behind lofty ideals.

# REEDS

Early reeds sprout like bamboos,
Slightly opened leaves look like rushes.
By the spring festival they will be enveloped in scales,
Then slowly the old roots will sprout hairs.
I have no love for the green of summer;
I love this decaying autumn.
Yellow leaves tumble in wind and rain,
Spots of white sway over rivers and lakes.
You cannot get to those lakes and rivers;
It is hard labor to transplant trees.
Silently a pair of wild ducks come flying;
All this becomes a painting.

## SUNG FU-KU'S EVENING LANDSCAPE OF THE HSIAO
## AND HSIANG RIVERS

The soldier stationed in the West recalls the lands of the South,
On the hall walls he paints the rivers, Hsiao and Hsiang.
In front of my eyes mountains in clouds emerge,
Wild water expands and floats in the empty space.
The old traveller thinks of his own province,
The faithful brush has forgotten all.
We can invite the sun in its orbit
To come and view this misty vision.

## By the Bank of Shou-yang[1]

There are green shelters, east and west of the lane;
Green lichens flourish to the north and south of the pool.
A lonely man comes with his dregs of wine.
How unexpected! The first call of the oriole!

久擁茅門客不來客
霜滿地凍蒼苔小齋
畢竟冬晴好催早
梅花一月開
光緒二酉夏楊伯潤

## A Poem

High and lofty, tiers of rock,
How solitary it stands.
Luckily, in this strong wind the green bamboos cluster;
Sun sets, no one about, seagulls have left.
Only the distant water remains,
Keeping company with the cold reeds.

# Su Ch'e

## While strolling below the T'ai-pai Mountains early in the morning, I wrote this poem on Ch'ung-shou Monastery following Tzu Ch'an's[1] rhyme

Morning glow below the mountain is no longer there;
Dewdrops have appeared on the tips of the forest trees.
Mountain peak peeps sidewise at the moon;
In country markets fires are lighted early.
Tree shadows still hide the magpie,
The hall is open and priests are at their meal.
Leaning on your pommel you should dream of me;
In the past we two rode one horse together.

## An Outing in Spring[1]

The ice has melted on the river, grass bank is green;
Few people have come out for a spring walk.
Floating bridge, drowned in water, cannot bear my weight;
Distilled wine in the village is no longer clear.
The winter flowers have sprouted their first buds under the pines,
In the ravine the lonely bird calls slowly for its mate.
Pulsating spring by the cave mouth bubbles out dragon's eyes;
Front court of the temple is sprouting duck's-tongue grass,
The pitcher flowers below the hills drip on children.
The scholar's family gathers on the mountaintop from whence comes the music.
The white silk skirts and the red-sleeved robes approach the river to see their
    reflections;
Blue-covered carriages with fine horses pass, resounding on the stone-paved road.
At dawn, with excited heart you try to arrive first;
Return not to your horse till you are really drunk.
I like it then when people leave and the west room is quiet;
Faint beams of the setting sun light up the touching trees.

## LIGHT SNOW AT THE SOUTH STREAM
## (FOLLOWING TZU CH'AN'S RHYME)

Night's snowfall at the South Stream ceases with dawn;
The guest leaves in the morning with wine still undigested.
Remaining snowflakes drifting in the wind chase the horse;
Light reflects on the frozen stream, unaware of the bridge.
Mountain is cold and frozen, no traveller goes there;
Long drinks make guests happy, dancing mood is high.
Returning on horseback we shall step over the jade-white snow;
From time to time I smell the forest and notice early shoots of plum branches.

## ASCENDING THE WANG-HAI TOWER
### (FOLLOWING TZU CH'AN'S RHYME)

Lotus leaves have just dried, paddy smells fragrant;
Startling thunder and rushing rain ushered in slight cold.
Blue evening sky slowly spreads the beauty of mountains in autumn,
Washing away the heavy make-up for a lighter one.

## Mountain village (following Tzu Ch'an's rhyme)

Roaming in the mountains,
It was pleasant to see the drooping wine-shop flags.
Limitless peach blossoms coupled with apricot flowers;
Ups and downs of this world make me want to avoid it
And take my family wandering as if I were homeless.

## SEEING THE LOTUS ON LIANG SHAN LAKE[1]
## I REMEMBER WU-HSING[2]

In the south, families speak of colored houseboats;
Water-lilies are near and far under a hazy sun.
I come across blossoming lotus in the Liang Shan Lake;
Suddenly I remember the ten *li* walk I took at Wu-hsing.

# White Heron Pavilion

The water in front of White Heron Island[1]
Rushes and scatters like alarmed horses and cows.
A pavilion so light that it appears to shake,
Boats pass carefully.
The rushing torrent crumbles the mountain,
So pure, like soft silk unfolded.
Who will be here for the mid-autumn festival?
Bright moon will shine full over the city.

## An evening drink at P'ei-hsien Pavilion

When the sun is about to set,
There will be more clouds and mist.
The night raven of the South range
Returns to northern hills.
City-wall towers are half bright, half dim;
Lighted lamps begin to cross the bridge.
The eighth month of the year,
It is still warm here in Kiangsi.
The banished official in the pavilion,
Whose hair is almost grey;
When will this confinement be over
And I can return free?
Near the bamboo fence
Are spread the yellow flowers and the white wine.

## In a boat amidst wind and snow

River surface is clean and pure,
Snow has not yet melted.
The skiff swings with the ripples,
Leaving no trace on the water.
O boatman, you need not pole so fast!
Let us watch every glorious peak of the Lu-shan Mountain.

## In imitation of a whistling tune from Su-chou

Fisherman! O fisherman!
Slight breeze and delicate rain on the water,
Raincoats made of green leaves, and yellow bamboo shoots.
Red wine and white fish do not return!
They never come back, never!
The long flute returns not,
From whence comes that single note?

# FOR THE FIRST TIME I SLOWLY ENTER THE HSÜAN RIVER

The traveller comes from afar,
Determined upon a long trip.
The low sail blends with the rivulet;
More clouds, and the sail is dampened by rain.
The boat stops in high reeds and mud;
Grass is green, ploughing cows are strong;
Deep in the village, seasonal birds twitter.
Unlike old T'ao[1] I am just appointed,
Thus I cannot write another "Returning Home."[2]

## POEMS OFFERED TO MY COLLEAGUE CHU DESCRIBING MY TRAVEL TO SHIH-CHAO IN THE DISTRICT OF CHI-CH'I[1]

### I

Travelling until the clear stream ends, we reach the dark blue peak;
Sombre precipice, blue mountain screen painted with pines.
This makes the traveller tarry at Shih-chao
And climb the blue mountains till the last range is reached.

### II

Rains clear and Shih-chao looks freshly polished,
Birds fly over, gibbons scratch about.
Old villagers pass by;
Suddenly I see the reflection of my dusty face,
I laugh at myself.
Why in recent years has my beard grown white?

# Huo-jan Pavilion

The city is in the south, the mountains in the north;
Every time I come here my spirit expands.
Blue tiles on a thousand houses freshly washed in rain;
Green pines in myriad gullies, fog just rising.
Throughout autumn I was ill in bed,
Listening to the sound of axes.
Today we ascend to the pavilion carrying our wine;
I request all of you to compose beautiful verses.
Allow me first to write this poem on the pavilion wall.

# HUI-HSIEN PAVILION

Northern ranges and southern screens
Exactly encircle all four directions.
Western mountains have a slight break
To let the rivulet flow.
Barbarians offer wine and entertain guests;
They know how wonderful these peaks are for travel.

## IN THE DEPTH OF SPRING

Red and green countryside turns darker green;
Behind closed doors I did not know that it is already late spring.
I am happy if my wild acres will grow more weeds.
Sitting here I watch the new shoots of bamboo
Closing the gaps in the forest.
Inside the bamboo curtain the flying catkins
Entwine in my broken dream.
Outside the window the singing oriole
Accompanies my lonely humming.
I wanted to hear the chanting of Surangama Sutra[1]
But was lazy and did not go.
The monk knew that I lack enlightenment.

# SAILING ON THE YI RIVER

In my youth when I went south,
I hated all boats.
On my return to level lands,
I cherished the memories of rivers and lakes.
Spring water submerges half the boat pole
With a thousand petals of flowers.
An eight-foot skiff, a jug of wine—
Slowly the boat drifted to the north of the city.
Now the plain is open and wide,
A little walk through a bamboo-covered path
And there is the little solitary pavilion.
Ministers of past regimes are difficult to obtain now,
Useless to lament the venerable elders!

Su Kuo

RHYMES IN THE MANNER OF THOSE OF YEH SHOU[1] ON THE
FESTIVAL OF TUAN-WU[2] BY THE WINDING
WATERS OF WEST LAKE

Hundreds of hidden springs sing amidst the grasses,
Already the rounded leafy covers of lotus are drooping,
As if wishing to seize the boat and sail away to distant waters.
The road that passes my gate is the road to the capital.

# Notes

## Hsü Hsüan (916–991)

Hsü was a native of Kuang-ling in Kiangsu province. Emperor T'ai-tsung appointed him the editor of a new corrected edition of Shuo Wen. He rose to be Supervising Censor but was ultimately banished to Pin-chou in Shensi province for neglecting his mother and committing adultery.

These poems are selected from Hsü Kung Chi, in Ssu-Pu-Pei-Yao. The Chinese titles and the folio and page numbers are given below.

1. Teng Kan-lu Szu pei wang. Folio 1, p. 4.
2. Ching-k'ou chiang chi nung shui. Folio 1, p. 4.
3. Ch'iu jih Lu-lung ts'un she. Folio 2, p. 6.
4. T'i Fu-kuei shan pei yü. Folio 3, pp. 9–10.
5. Fu te ch'iu chiang wan chao. Folio 6, p. 6.
6. Ho Ch'en Hsi-ma Shan Chuang-hsin Chüan. Folio 4, p. 6.
7. Ch'iu jih fan chou fu p'in hua. Folio 5, p. 8.
8. Ho Chung ta-chien fan chou t'ung yu chien shih. Folio 5, p. 7.
9. Ho Chang shao-chien chou chung wang Chiang Shan. Folio 5, p. 8.
10. Yu t'i Pai-lu chou chiang ou sung Ch'en chün. Folio 5, p. 10.

### NOTES

P. 13  [1] "Sweet-dew," or the Chinese equivalent of the Buddhist-Sanskrit word "Amrita."
      [2] Nanking (side of the city which is by the river).
      [3] Islet on the Yangtze River near the sea.
      [4] Nanking.
16  [1] Refers to T'ao Ch'ien's (365–427) famous poem (fu) "Kuei ch'ü lai."
20  [1] Superintendent.
21  [1] Superintendent.
      [2] His friend's name.
22  [1] Riches and fame.

## Lin Pu (967–1028)

Lin Pu, a native of Ch'ien-t'ang in Chekiang province, became a hermit early in his life and lived alone on Lone Hill, a small hill situated in West Lake near the city of Hangchow. He never married. He referred to his plum trees as his "wives" and his pet cranes as his "sons." He threw away his poems and did not care for fame. His friends managed to preserve some three hundred poems. After his death he was buried by his cottage with his last poem by his side.

These poems are selected from Ho Ch'ing Shih Chi, in Ssu-Pu-Pei-Yao. The Chinese titles and the folio and page numbers are given below.

1. Hu lou wan wang. Folio 1, p. 1.
2. Ch'iu jih hsi hu hsien fan. Folio 1, p. 1.
3. Pei shan hsieh wang. Folio 1, p. 3.
4. Shan ts'un tung mu. Folio 1, p. 4.
5. Hu Shang yin chü. Folio 2, p. 1.
6. Ch'ih yang shan chü. Folio 2, p. 6.
7. Chu lin. Folio 4, p. 2.

8. *Yi-ts'ung shih shan t'ing. Folio 4, p. 3.*
9. *Ch'iu chiang hsieh wang. Folio 4, pp. 3–4*
10. *Ch'eng-kung ch'iao tso. Folio 4, p. 4.*

## NOTES

P. 27  ¹ A recluse perhaps.
 29  ¹ Old Chinese name for India.
 30  ¹ Sign of a hostelry.
 31  ¹ Sheath which covers the joints of the bamboo.
 34  ¹ A student of the Northern Sung artist, Tung Yüan (907–960). Chü-jan (*c.* 975) was famous for his landscapes with heavy ink-work.

## Mei Yao-ch'en (1002–1060)

*Mei Yao-ch'en, a native of Wan-ling in Anhui province, is considered to be a poet who perfected the poetry of his time by following the attitude of "p'ing-tan"—tranquil ease. He rose to be a minor official in the Ministry of Justice. Ou-yang Hsiu, the prime minister and the literary genius of his time, was Mei's greatest admirer. When at the age of fifty-nine Mei, a poor official, died of plague, Ou-yang said, "It is not that poetry makes paupers of men, but nearly always men must first become paupers before they can write good poetry."*

*These poems are selected from* Wan Ling Chi, *vols, 1-6 in Ssu-Pu-Pei-Yao. The Chinese titles and the folio and page numbers are given below.*

1. *Yu Lung-men tzu Ch'ien-ch'i kuo Pao-ying ching she. Folio 1, p. 2.*
2. *Ling yün. Folio 1, p. 3.*
3. *Yü chu yu p'u Ming-yüan T'ing na liang fen t'i. Folio 1, p. 8.*
4. *Ho Hsi-shen pi shu Hsiang-shan Szu. Folio 2, p. 2.*
5. *Ho Hsi-shen wan fan yi ch'uan. Folio 2, p. 2.*
6. *Kung-lu chien. Folio 2, p. 6.*
7. *Tzu Chün-chi Chung Yüan pu teng T'ai-shih chung feng. Folio 2, p. 6.*
8. *Tsao tu Ch'ang-lu Chiang. Folio 3, p. 8.*
9. *Hsin chi teng Chou-wang ch'eng. Folio 7, p. 3.*
10. *T'ien chia. Folio 7, p. 3.*
11. *Lu-shan shan hsing. Folio 7, pp. 5–6.*
12. *Yü. Folio 17, p. 7.*
13. *Ch'ing. Folio 17, p. 7.*
14. *Yi yün ho Tzu-cheng shih lang hsüeh hou teng K'an-shan T'ing. Folio 26, p. 3.*
15. *Yüan shan. Folio 28, p. 1.*
16. *Lien t'ang. Folio 28, p. 1.*
17. *Yü t'an. Folio 28, p. 1.*
18. *T'ao hsi. Folio 28, p. 1.*
19. *T'ai ching. Folio 28, p. 1.*
20. *Ch'uan shang t'ien chia. Folio 34, p. 5.*
21. *Kuo Yen Chou. Folio 37, p. 9.*
22. *Yin-ching Shan fang Huai-hsien shang jen pu yü. Folio 42, p. 1.*
23. *Ch'iu jih chia chü. Folio 42, p. 2.*
24. *Yeh wang. Folio 43, p. 8.*

25. *Hsien Fu-kuo. Folio 43, p. 8.*
26. *Erh yüeh wu jih hsüeh. Folio 51, p. 7.*
27. *Yi ch'uan. Folio 58, p. 3.*

## NOTES

P. 39   ¹ Buddhist recitations, always chanted.

   42   ¹ This refers to Yüan-shu (T. Kung-lu) who fought with Ts'ao Ts'ao and was defeated by Liu Pei. He died in A.D. 199.

   43   ¹ A mountain in Honan province.

   44   ¹ Yangtze River (?).
        ² Nanking.

   45   ¹ Thorny trees about 15 feet high, whose leaves are used for feeding silkworms before the mulberry leaves are ready.

   50   ¹ A vice-president of the Six Boards: Civil office, Rites, Revenue, War, Punishments, and Works.

   56   ¹ See note to p. 45.

   62   ¹ This refers to the famous saying of Chuang-tzu about his becoming a butterfly in a dream.

## Ou-yang Hsiu (1007–1072)

*Ou-yang was a native of Lu-ling in Kiangsi province. He lost his father when he was four and was brought up by his mother, who taught him to read and write. He was the mastermind behind the downfall of the Hsi-k'un style of imitation T'ang poetry that was prevalent between 960 and 1000 during the beginning of the Northern Sung. Ou-yang Hsiu and Mei Yao-ch'en together rejected this highly ornate literature, labeled it decadent and lacking in thought. They created the literature of their own time, a literature of greater depth and content. The literary ideals they established remained the ideals of Chinese literature till they came under attack in the 1920's when the pai-hua or colloquial literature came to the forefront.*

*Ou-yang made significant contributions to the entire field of Chinese culture, including poetry, prose, historiography, classical studies and archaeology. It was his breadth of talent that ultimately made him prime minister under Emperor Jen-tsung.*

*These poems are selected from Ou-yang Wen Chung Ch'uan Chi, vols. 1–7, in Ssu-Pu-Pei-Yao. The Chinese titles and the folio and page numbers are given below.*

1. *Shang shan. Folio 1, p. 2.*
2. *Hsia shan. Folio 1, p. 2.*
3. *Shang Fang Ko. Folio 1, p. 2.*
4. *Yi ch'uan fan chou. Folio 1, p. 2.*
5. *Tzu P'u-t'i pu yüeh kuei Kuang-hua Ssu. Folio 1, p. 3.*
6. *Shih-p'ing lu. Folio 3, p. 9.*
7. *Yü hou tu hsing Lo pei. Folio 10, p. 2.*
8. *Yüan shan. Folio 10, p. 7.*
9. *Feng-lo T'ing yu ch'un san shou. Folio 11, p. 6.*
10. *Huai Sung Lou hsin k'ai nan hsüan yü chün liao hsiao yin. Folio 11, p. 7.*
11. *T'ien chia. Folio 11, p. 7.*

12. *Ch'u chih Ying-chou Hsi Hu chung jui lien huang yang chi Huai-nan chuan yün Lü Tu-chih fa yün Hsü Chu-k'o. Folio 11, p. 9.*
13. *Yi-yüan ch'iao (San ch'iao shih). Folio 11, p. 9.*
14. *Feng shih tao chung wu yen ch'ang yün. Folio 12, p. 6.*
15. *Chi t'i Sha-ch'i Pao-hsi Yüan. Folio 14, p. 3.*
16. *Tzu Chün-chi Chung Yüan pu teng T'ai-shih Chung feng. Folio 51, p. 3.*
17. *Chün-chi Ssu. Folio 51, p. 4.*
18. *Chung feng. Folio 51, p. 4.*
19. *Wan po Yüeh-yang. Folio 52, p. 9.*
20. *T'i Ch'u-chou Tsui Weng T'ing. Folio 53, p. 9.*
21. *Hsüeh ch'ing. Folio 54, p. 4.*
22. *Hsi yüan. Folio 54, p. 4.*
23. *Wan pu Lü-yin yüan sui teng Ning-ts'ui T'ing. Folio 54, p. 6.*
24. *Lou t'ou. Folio 55, p. 1.*
25. *Ho-lung Men hsiao wang. Folio 55, p. 8.*
26. *Yi ch'uan tu yu. Folio 56, p. 3.*
27. *Chi hou k'an yün tsou pi ch'eng Yüan Chen p'an-kuan erh shou. Folio 56, p. 5.*
28. *Ho Sheng Yü Pai-hua Chou erh shou. Folio 56, p. 6.*
29. *Hua-chou Kuei-yen T'ing. Folio 56, p. 7.*
30. *Hsi Hu fan chou ch'eng Yün-shih hsüeh shih Chang Shan. Folio 56, p. 9.*
31. *Tiao che. Folio 57, p. 5.*
32. *Ho yeh. Folio 57, p. 5.*
33. *Ch'u hsia Hsi Hu. Folio 57, p. 10.*

## NOTES

P. 72   [1] The road probably faced a flat stony cliff with pictorial patterns of rock veins, similar to the stone plaques in marble and other stones that are so much admired by Chinese for their natural pictorial veins.

73   [1] River in Honan province.
      [2] A mountain in Honan province.
      [3] Near the Sung range in Honan province.

76   [1] Pavilion where one longs for the Sung mountains.

77   [1] The Chinese soil-god.

78   [1] In modern Anhui province.
      [2] In modern Anhui province.

80   [1] Two wooden rollers are used in China to hold paintings as they hang straight down on the wall. Heavy rollers prevent wind from swinging the painting to and fro.

81   [1] Han Wu-ti's envoy in the Hsiung-nu lands. He was captured and imprisoned by the Hsiung-nus for nineteen years but remained faithful and constant to the Han emperors.

82   [1] A stream in Fukien province.

83   [1] A mountain in Honan province.

86   [1] Near T'ai-yüan in Shansi.

87   [1] Ch'u-chou is in Anhui province.

91   [1] Probably Ch'u-hsin in Shensi province.
      [2] P'u-ch'eng hsien in Shensi.

93   [1] A river in Honan province.

94   [1] A judicial title.

95 ¹ Southeast of the city of Teng-hsien in Honan province.
97 ¹ Commissioner of Transport.

## Su Shun-ch'in (1008–1048)

*Su was a native of Tzu-chou in Szechwan province. He was a brilliant student and graduated with a chin-shih degree at the age of twenty-one. He held a position in the Chin-tsou-yüan, distributing edicts and memorials to proper authorities. He was impeached for selling waste paper from the office trash cans and using the money to hire female entertainers and for holding a drinking party in the office. He retired early to his villa, the Sea Blue Pavilion at Suchow in the province of Kiangsu. He was extremely interested in military matters and was a very sought-after calligraphist in the "grass" script.*

*These poems are selected from Su Hsüeh-shih Chi, vol. 1, in Ssu-Pu-Pei-Yao. The Chinese titles and the folio and page numbers are given below.*

1. *Chin-shan Szu. Folio 4, pp. 6–7.*
2. *Chiu yüeh wu jih yeh ch'u p'an men po yü hu chien ou ch'eng mi hui tso shang shu ch'eng Huang yü. Folio 4, pp. 6–7.*
3. *Ch'un jih wan ch'ing. Folio 6, p. 2.*
4. *Tu Yu Wang-ch'uan. Folio 6, p. 4.*
5. *Liu t'i Fan-ch'uan Li chang kuan chuang. Folio 6, p. 4.*
6. *Hsin-k'ai Hu wan chi. Folio 7, p. 3.*
7. *Yang-chou ch'eng nan yen pin t'ing. Folio 8, p. 4.*

### NOTES

P. 104 ¹ Name of a courtesan: Green moth.
      ² Bitter herbs and seafood, probably used as appetizers.
   105 ¹ For building their nests.
   106 ¹ T'ang dynasty poet-painter Wang Wei's villa was at Wang-ch'uan in Shensi province.
   107 ¹ East of the old capital of Ch'ang-an in Shensi. Once the poet Tu Fu resided here.
      ² Located near Fan-ch'uan.
   109 ¹ A town in Kiangsu province.

## Tseng Kung (1019–1083)

*Tseng has been considered one of the best prose writers of his period. Following Ou-yang Hsiu and Su Shih, he has been traditionally considered one of the great masters of the soft (yin) quality in writing. He was a pupil of Ou-yang Hsiu but never hesitated to challenge his master's overreaching rationalizations. Tseng Kung was instrumental in introducing Wang An-shih to Ou-yang Hsiu, great political rivals but admirers of each other's literary work. Tseng Kung travelled as a minor administrator in many provinces, and as he travelled he composed poems on nature. His poetry has always been overshadowed by his prose, but these poems possess a strong emotional character that distinguishes Tseng Kung from his contemporaries.*

*These poems are selected from Yüan-Feng-Lei-Kao, in Ssu-Pu-Pei-Yao. The Chinese titles and page numbers are given below.*

1. *Yung hsüeh. Folio 2, p. 3.*
2. *Yu Lang-yeh Shan. Folio 2, p. 11.*

3. *T'ao hua yüan. Folio 3, p. 2.*
4. *Pan-shan T'ing. Folio 3, p. 2.*
5. *Chao-yin Szu. Folio 5, p. 5.*
6. *Cheng yüeh liu jih hsüeh chi. Folio 7, p. 5.*
7. *Ch'iao-shan T'ing. Folio 7, p. 3.*
8. *Hsi Hu na liang. Folio 7, p. 5.*
9. *Chün lou. Folio 7, p. 9.*
10. *Li Ch'i-chou hou wu shou. Folio 7, pp. 9–10, Nos. 1–3 and 5.*
11. *Kan-lu Szu To-ching Lou. Folio 7, p. 10.*
12. *Ch'u chiao. Folio 8, p. 7.*
13. *Hsi Lou. Folio 8, p. 8.*
14. *Ch'eng nan erh shou. Folio 8, p. 8.*

## NOTES

P. 114    [1] Tsing-chou Fu in the eastern part of Shantung. This name is often applied to the whole promontory.

    [2] K'ung Ch'iu (Confucius) and Yen Hui, ancient sages.

116    [1] A pavilion half way up the mountain.

119    [1] Ch'iao-shan range (Magpie Mountain), in Li-ch'eng county of Shantung province.

    [2] Poet Tu Fu.

    [3] Poet himself.

122    [1] In Li-ch'eng county of Shantung province.

124    [1] The autumn festival.

## Ssu-ma Kuang (1019–1086)

*Ssu-ma Kuang's fame rests mainly on the fact that he was the opponent of the "innovator" Wang An-shih and wrote the great history of China, Tzu Chih T'ung Chien. He became minister of state under Emperor Jen Tsung. He resigned in 1070, but returned to active politics in 1085. He fell ill and died in 1086.*

*The poems are selected from Ssu-ma Wen Kung Chi, vol. 3, in Ssu-Pu-Pei-Yao. The Chinese titles and the folio and page numbers are given below.*

1. *Hsien lou. Folio 12, p. 5.*
2. *Liu. Folio 12, p. 5.*

## Wang An-shih (1021–1086)

*Wang An-shih's fame rests on the controversial economic and political reforms that he undertook during the reign of Emperor Shen-tsung (1068–1085). As a young scholar he was greatly acclaimed by Ou-yang Hsiu, although later Ou-yang strongly opposed Wang's reforms. Wang An-shih was a great admirer of the T'ang poet Tu Fu and was undoubtedly influenced by his poetic qualities, particularly Tu Fu's love and concern for the common people. Wang certainly admired Tu Fu's lyricism also. He compiled an anthology of T'ang poetry and held strong opinions on poetry which he expressed vigorously in his remarks on literary criticism. He wrote voluminously and, with the exception of Ou-yang Hsiu and Su Shih, was perhaps the most important literary figure of his time.*

*These poems are selected from* Lin-Ch'uan-Chi, *in* Ssu-Pu-Pei-Yao. *The Chinese titles and the folio and page numbers are given below.*

1. *Chi shih erh shou. Folio 3, p. 3, No. 1.*
2. *T'ai-pai Ling. Folio 13, p. 5.*
3. *Pan-shan ch'un wan chi shih. Folio 14, p. 3.*
4. *Tung-yang tao chung. Folio 15, p. 3.*
5. *Tzu Pai-t'u Ts'un ju Pei Szu erh shou. Folio 15, pp. 7–8, No. 1.*
6. *K'un Shan Hui-chü Szu tz'u Chang Hu yün. Folio 16, p. 4.*
7. *Yu Hang-chou Sheng-kuo Szu. Folio 16, p. 5.*
8. *Ch'un feng. Folio 19, p. 3.*
9. *Chiang shang. Folio 26, p. 6.*
10. *Hsi Tai-yi Kung Lou. Folio 26, p. 10.*
11. *Ch'iu yün. Folio 27, pp. 6–7.*
12. *Mu mo. Folio 27, p. 7.*
13. *Ch'un feng. Folio 27, p. 7.*
14. *Po ch'uan Kua Chou. Folio 29, p. 9.*
15. *Chin-ling chi shih san shou. Folio 30, p. 3, No. 1.*
16. *Ch'eng pei. Folio 30, p. 4.*
17. *Kuan Ming-chou t'u. Folio 30, p. 4.*
18. *Chung Shan chi shih. Folio 30, p. 5.*
19. *Chiang shang. Folio 30, p. 9.*
20. *Ting-lin suo chü. Folio 30, p. 10.*
21. *Ch'un jih. Folio 31, p. 7.*
22. *Hsing hua. Folio 33, p. 3.*
23. *Ch'u ching. Folio 34, p. 5.*
24. *Ch'u Chin-ling. Folio 34, p. 6.*

## NOTES

P. 133  [1] In Honan province.

134  [1] In Honan province.

135  [1] Honan province.

[2] The sense of inactive quietude, the opposite of the active *yang* feeling; based on the *yin yang* theory of action and inaction.

136  [1] A town in Shantung province.

[2] Kiangsu province.

[3] Provinces of Hupeh and Hunan.

138  [1] In Kiangsu province.

139  [1] A town by the Fuchun River in Chekiang province.

144  [1] A variety of coarse rice (?)

146  [1] The part of the Grand Canal on the Yangtze River, the present Chinkiang city in Kiangsu province.

[2] In Honan province.

147  [1] See note to p. 156.

149  [1] East of Yin-hsien county in Chekiang province.

150  [1] In Honan province.

152  [1] Ting-lin-chen, a town in Kiangsu province, situated to the east of Kiang-ning county.

156  [1] City of Nanking.

# Su Shih (1036–1101)

Su Shih, the greatest of the Sung poets, is better known by his fancy name Su Tung-p'o. He was born in the district of Mei-shan in Szechwan province. Su Shih received his chin-shih degree in 1057 and was examined by Ou-yang Hsiu and Mei Yao-ch'en. A disciple of these famous poets and scholars, Su developed a brilliant and easy approach to poetry and a rather conservative attitude towards politics. He became one of the opponents of Wang An-shih's "reforms." He rose very high in office under several emperors and was banished under others. It is remarkable that the two banishments Su underwent were responsible for the best poems of the poet.

These poems are selected from Tung-p'o Ch'i Chi, in Ssu-Pu-Pei-Yao. The Chinese titles and the page numbers are given below.

Volume 1:

1. Lung Szu. Folio 1, p. 10.
2. Ta-ch'in Szu. Folio 2, p. 3.
3. Liu yüeh erh shih ch'i jih Wang-hu Lou tsui shu. Folio 3, p. 7.
4. Wang-hai Lou wan ching wu chüeh. Folio 3, p. 10.
5. Yin hu shang ch'u ching hou yü erh shou. Folio 4, p. 7.
6. Shan ts'ün wu chüeh. Folio 4, p. 8.
7. Hsin-ch'eng tao chung erh shou. Folio 4, p. 8, No. 1.
8. Han-lu kang. Folio 7, p. 7.
9. Li Szu-hsün hua Ch'ang Chiang chüeh tao t'u. Folio 10, p. 2.
10. T'i Hsi-lin pi. Folio 13, p. 11.
11. Teng yün-lung Shan. Folio 10, p. 3.
12. Hui-ts'ung ch'un chiang hsiao ching erh shou. Folio 15, p. 10, No. 1.
13. Tzu Hsing-kuo wang Yün su Shih-t'ien yi nan erh shih wu li yeh jen she. Folio 13, p. 8.
14. Tz'u yün Ts'an Liao t'ung ch'ien. Folio 18, p. 14.
15. Kuo Hsi hua ch'iu shan p'ing yüan. Folio 16, p. 10.
16. Shu Li Shih-nan suo hua ch'iu ching. Folio 16, p. 11.

Volume 2:

17. Huai shang tsao fa. Folio 2, p. 5.
18. Chiang-hsi yi shou. Folio 4, p. 6.
19. Liu t'i Hsien-sheng Szu yi shou. Folio 7, p. 7.
20. Pi-lo Tung yi shou. Folio 4, p. 8.
21. Shih yi yüeh erh shih liu jih Sung Feng T'ing hsia mei hua sheng k'ai. Folio 4, p. 10.
22. Tsai yung ch'ien yün yi shou. Folio 4, pp. 10–11.
23. Yu Po-lo Hsiang-ch'i Szu yi shou. Folio 5, p. 3.
24. Lien yü chiang chang erh shou. Folio 5, p. 4.
25. San yüeh erh shih chiu jih erh shou. Folio 6, p. 3.
26. Teng-mai-yi T'ung-ch'ao ko erh shou. Folio 7, p. 1.

Volume 4:

27. Ling shang fang tao jen pu yü. Folio 1, p. 1.
28. Kuo Yi-pin chien yi chung luan shan. Folio 1, p. 10.
29. Chiang shang k'an shan. Folio 1, p. 11.
30. Lu. Folio 1, p. 22.
31. Ju hsia. Folio 2, p. 4.
32. Sung Fu-ku hua Hsiao Hsiang wan ching t'u san shou. Folio 2, p. 6, No. 1.

226

33. *Shou-yang an hsia. Folio 2, p. 22.*
34. *Chüeh chü erh shou. Folio 2, p. 26.*

## NOTES

P. 160   [1] A Nestorian Christian monastery near Sian.

163   [1] A famous beauty of the fifth century.

165   [1] A mountain in Kansu, where there is a cave into which the sun is said to sink at night.

169   [1] A mountain in Kiangsu province.

     [2] Yellow water-mallows; probably the cliff is so named because of the strewn boulders.

     [3] The poet; this is his title as a commissioner.

170   [1] A Buddhist monk and painter (*c.* 1070). He is noted for his water-birds and miniatures.

173   [1] Kuo Hsi (*c.* 1020–1090), an academician of the Art Academy (Hua-yüan) famous for his landscapes with high perspective and involutions.

     [2] Yi River in Honan province.

     [3] The beautiful Sung dynasty city on the Yellow River.

     [4] A tributary of the Yellow River.

     [5] The famous gorge of the Yi River.

178   [1] The capital of the Jade Emperor (Taoist myth).

     [2] A friend or relative of the poet.

180   [1] In Fukien province.

181   [1] In Kwangtung province.

     [2] The Tao.

182   [1] A ridge of Yüeh-hsiu Mountains in Kwangtung province.

184   [1] A postal station at Kiungchow, Hainan island.

     [2] A famous physician of antiquity, said to have been able to raise the dead.

186   [1] A county in Szechwan province.

188   [1] Modern provinces of Hupeh, Hunan, and Szechwan.

     [2] Two ancient legendary men of wisdom who disappeared in the West: P'eng Tsu and Lao Tzu (Lao Tan).

     [3] Meng Ch'ang, the second sovereign of the Later Shu State who surrendered to the Sung sovereign and Yü Yen.

192   [1] In Shansi province.

## *Su Ch'e (1039–1112)*

*Su Ch'e was Su Shih's younger brother; he graduated as a* chin-shih *along with his brother in 1057. He also opposed Wang An-shih's "reforms," and like his brother was twice dismissed to minor posts in the provinces. He was a devotee of Yogic breathing exercises and greatly influenced Su Shih, who, influenced by Su Ch'e, became interested in Buddhist and Taoist mystic practices.*

*These poems are selected from* Luan-Ch'eng-Chi, *in* Ssu-Pu-Pei-Yao. *The Chinese titles and the folio and page numbers are given below.*

*Volume 1:*

1. *Tz'u yün Tzu Ch'an T'ai-pai Shan hsia tsao hsing t'i Chung-shou Yüan. Folio 1, p. 11.*
2. *T'a ching. Folio 1, p. 14.*
3. *Tz'u yün Tzu Ch'an nan ch'i wei hsüeh. Folio 2, p. 13.*

4. *Tz'u yün Tzu Ch'an teng Wang-hai Lou wu chüeh. Folio 12, pp. 12–13, No. 4.*
5. *Tz'u yün Tzu Ch'an shan ts'un wu chüeh. Folio 5, p. 2, No. 1.*
6. *Liang Shan p'o chien ho hua yi Wu-hsing wu chüeh. Folio 6, p. 9, No. 1.*
7. *Pai-lu T'ing. Folio 10, p. 1.*
8. *P'ei-hsien T'ing wan yin. Folio 12, p. 3.*
9. *Chou chung feng hsüeh wu chüeh. Folio 12, p. 11, No. 5.*
10. *Hsiao wen Su-chou tiao hsiao tz'u erh shou. Folio 13, p. 13, No. 1.*
11. *Tz'u yün ch'ih ch'u ju Hsüan Ho. Folio 13, p. 13.*
12. *Ch'u tao Chi-ch'i shih shih san jih ch'u ch'eng nan yeh erh tz'u yu Shih-chao ou ch'eng szu hsiao shih ch'eng Chu T'ung kuan. Folio 13, p. 14, Nos. 3 and 4.*

*Volume 2:*
13. *Huo-jan T'ing. Folio 14, p. 4.*
14. *Hui-hsien Kuan erh chüeh chü. Folio 16, p. 11, No. 1.*
*Volume 4:*
15. *Ch'un shen san shou. Folio 4, p. 9, No. 1.*
16. *Fan Yi shui yi shou. Folio 3, p. 12.*

### NOTES

P. 197   ¹ Su Tung-p'o (Su Shih).

198   ¹ A poem recording local customs sent to Tzu Ch'an (Su Shih).

202   ¹ Lake below the Liang Shan Mountains in Shantung Province.

      ² A county in Fukien province.

203   ¹ An island in the Yangtze River, in Kiangsu province.

207   ¹ The poet T'ao Ch'ien (365–427).

      ² A famous poem by T'ao Ch'ien.

208   ¹ In Anhui province.

211   ¹ A popular Buddhist discourse.

## Su Kuo (1072–1123)

*Su Kuo was the third son of Su Shih and was his father's constant companion during Su Shih's banishment to Hainan island. Under the guidance of his father, Su Kuo rapidly developed into a poet and painter. He was invited by Emperor Hui-tsung to paint rocks and bamboos in one of the new palaces.*

*This poem is selected from* Hsieh Ch'uan Chi, *in* Ssu-Pu-Pei-Yao. *The Chinese title and the folio and page number are given below.*

1. *Tz'u yün Yeh Shou tuan-wu hsi hu ch'ü shui. Folio 3, p. 14.*

### NOTES

P. 215   ¹ Governor Yeh.

      ² The fifth day of the fifth month when the poet Ch'ü Yüan committed suicide by jumping in the Mi-lo River during the reign of King Huai (328–299 B.C.) of the royal house of Ch'u.